"Your project to write the remembrance of your grandmother has much more importance than you will ever know."

—JAMES M. HOUSTON
Professor Emeritus of Spiritual Theology, Regent College

"I was quickly drawn into the story and the touching life-long devotion of the author's family members to each other and their sustaining faith. Their solid foundation of love and commitment surfaces as they prioritize their lives for the end-of-life journey of the two matriarchs. A special gift emerges and surprises the author when she makes personal sacrifices to care for her mother."

—MARTHA GOLAY
Hospice bereavement coordinator, retired

"It is a rare gift for someone to be so intellectually gifted and so emotionally vulnerable. Through this story, Mary will take you through beauty, discovery, fear, and grief. It is a beautiful and stirring work."

—SEAN STEVENSON-DOUGLAS
President, Eston College

"In the refreshingly frank style of Corrie Ten Boom's inner dialogue, Mary Katherine Hom-Smith's travelogue carries us through her phases of maturing in Christ. In the particulars of her story, we learn general truths about generational faithfulness to God, dependence on the real and convincing work of the Holy Spirit, and familial belonging within the catholic community of Christ. Mary Katherine serves a rich portion of theological reflections through the particulars of her family's story. Let the reader feast."

—DRU JOHNSON
Templeton Senior Research Fellow, Wycliffe Hall, Oxford University

"Mary's book, *When Grandma Looked at the Moon*, offers a tender glimpse into three generations of women bound by profound love. Their connection—from sharing quiet moments in Yosemite, to her grandmother's faithful prayer during Mary's mission trips—transcends generations and geography. Learning about their relationship, I was moved by how Mary cared for her grandmother in her final chapters, reminding us that sometimes the greatest adventure is coming home to those who matter most."

—ANN CHOW
Consultant, Adaptive Leaders

"Hom-Smith's heartfelt narrative weaves two powerful threads. First, it blends a deeply personal journey of faith and grief with inspiring accounts of travel and service. Second, through the author's experience accompanying her mother and grandmother in their final stages of life, readers are invited into a moving story of familial love and sisterhood in Christ, along with a powerful testimony of three generations of women led by the Spirit. A must-read, profoundly moving, and spiritually enriching."

—ELŻBIETA ŁAZAREWICZ-WYRZYKOWSKA
Visiting Lecturer, Margaret Beaufort Institute of Theology, Cambridge, United Kingdom

When Grandma Looked at the Moon

When Grandma Looked at the Moon

A Memoir of Generations, Faith, and Life

MARY KATHERINE Y. H. HOM-SMITH

RESOURCE *Publications* • Eugene, Oregon

WHEN GRANDMA LOOKED AT THE MOON
A Memoir of Generations, Faith, and Life

Copyright © 2025 Mary Katherine Y. H. Hom-Smith. All rights reserved. Except for brief quotations in critical publications or reviews, no part of this book may be reproduced in any manner without prior written permission from the publisher. Write: Permissions, Wipf and Stock Publishers, 199 W. 8th Ave., Suite 3, Eugene, OR 97401.

Resource Publications
An Imprint of Wipf and Stock Publishers
199 W. 8th Ave., Suite 3
Eugene, OR 97401

www.wipfandstock.com

PAPERBACK ISBN: 979-8-3852-4311-2
HARDCOVER ISBN: 979-8-3852-4312-9
EBOOK ISBN: 979-8-3852-4313-6

VERSION NUMBER 031425

Some names and details have been changed or combined to protect the privacy and anonymity of individuals involved. All else is true as I experienced it.

All Scripture quotations, unless otherwise indicated, are taken from the Holy Bible, New International Version®, NIV®. Copyright ©1973, 1978, 1984, 2011 by Biblica, Inc.™ Used by permission of Zondervan. All rights reserved worldwide. www.zondervan.com The "NIV" and "New International Version" are trademarks registered in the United States Patent and Trademark Office by Biblica, Inc.™

Scripture quotations marked ESV are from the ESV® Bible (The Holy Bible, English Standard Version®), © 2001 by Crossway, a publishing ministry of Good News Publishers. Used by permission. All rights reserved. The ESV text may not be quoted in any publication made available to the public by a Creative Commons license. The ESV may not be translated in whole or in part into any other language.

Interior illustration of Half Dome with moon: © Atlas C. K. Cox. Used with permission.

In Memory of

Grandma
and
Mom

With Gratitude to

Uncle Albert
Lyn and Bill
Fr. Maximos
Onesimus
Muzoora
Geoff
Alice
Steph
Innocent
St. Seraphim
and
St. Parthenios

And for

Nate

And God made the two great lights—the greater light to rule the day and the lesser light to rule the night—and the stars.

—Genesis 1:16 (ESV)

But enough on the greatness of the sun and moon. May He Who has given us intelligence to recognise in the smallest objects of creation the great wisdom of the Contriver make us find in great bodies a still higher idea of their Creator. However, compared with their Author, the sun and moon are but a fly and an ant. The whole universe cannot give us a right idea of the greatness of God; and it is only by signs, weak and slight in themselves, often by the help of the smallest insects and of the least plants, that we raise ourselves to Him. Content with these words let us offer our thanks, I to Him who has given me the ministry of the Word, you to Him who feeds you with spiritual food. . . . May He feed you for ever, and in proportion to your faith grant you the manifestation of the Spirit in Jesus Christ our Lord, to whom be glory and power for ever and ever. Amen.

—St. Basil of Caesarea, sermon on "The Creation of Luminous Bodies"[1]

---

1. Basil of Caesarea, "Creation of Luminous Bodies," 89.

Contents

1 Vancouver and Seattle | 1
2 Calgary | 16
3 Mosta | 34
4 Drumheller | 40
5 Sacramento I | 50
6 Johannesburg, Gaborone, and the Mozambican–Northern Zimbabwean Border | 60
7 Sacramento II | 87
8 Christmas Day, 2013 | 99
9 The Zoo | 106
10 The Outskirts of Musanze | 108
11 Mom | 126
12 Miki | 135
13 A Birthday in Yosemite | 142
14 Nate | 147
15 Epilogue | 156

Illustration | 161
Postscript | 163
Acknowledgments | 165
Bibliography | 167
About the Author | 168

1

Vancouver and Seattle

IT WAS ONE OF those rare sunny days in Vancouver, when the sunlight hit the walls of our low-budget apartment so that they glowed the color of pale salmonberries. A thick waft of white steam unfurled and rose up from an old enamel pot in the tiny kitchen, and I could hear my lunch boiling and burbling away its excitement that the beans I had soaked overnight—a simple and frequent staple while living on a seminary student income—were finally cooked and ready. I darted up from the stacks of theology books I was enmeshed in, and in five swift steps was nearly at the dilapidated stove. My environment may not have been posh by a longshot, but my inside felt as light and free as the sunlight and my still-bubbling meal. For four years, I had studied what I loved: the Christian Scriptures. Yet, there was something rewarding in knowing that I was working on the final term paper of the final course for my Master of Divinity (MDiv) degree. Though I would not be completely done with my studies at Regent—I had taken so many extra courses while studying for an MDiv that I was also halfway through an advanced master's degree (Master of Theology, ThM)—with the submission of my final MDiv paper, the only thing I would lack for a ThM degree was a thesis, and I was more eager than the steam over my pot of beans to rise and dive into research for that.

And then there was a loud, clanging burst of ringing—that weighty, universal '90s experience of the unexpected phone call. *Brrr-ring, brr-ing!*

Flick off the slightly loose plastic knob on the stove and leap for the phone. "Hello!" I shouted breathlessly as I grabbed the receiver.

"Mary..."

I froze. It was my mom, and I knew that tone of voice, though I had rarely heard it. How she always managed to communicate so much to me in just one or two words or even just a look was always a small wonder to me. I felt my weight shift as my feet planted themselves on the ground and I tucked the phone's receiver under my ear. "Hi, Mom. What's wrong?"

"Grandma's in the hospital."

"Oh no! Wait—how do you know?" My mom lived in Sacramento, but Grandma usually lived in Asia doing Christian service work, occasionally returning to the United States for furlough.

"She's been staying with Uncle Peter and Auntie Sarah in Seattle for furlough, and they said that a couple days ago she had heart pain. She was in so much pain that she cried—"

"Grandma never cries!"

"—and then she called Auntie Lillian in Fresno, who cried because Grandma was crying—"

"Auntie Lillian never cries!"

"—Uncle Gene heard Auntie Lillian crying while she was on the phone with Grandma, and he started crying!"

"Are you kidding me? Uncle Gene *never* cries!"

"So now Grandma's in the hospital, and we don't know what's going to happen. She's refusing food and water. You know what they say about when people stop eating and drinking."

"No—what?"

"They're ready to die. Your grandma on Dad's side did that shortly before she died."

I was silent, thinking hard... for two seconds. I loved my studies and was nearly done with my MDiv degree, but I loved my Grandma more. She was hundreds of miles away from my Mom, my crying aunt, and my very surprisingly crying uncle. More relatives were in Seattle, but they were working full time and the weekend was five days away. Where I was, in a quiet corner of Vancouver, was not very close to Seattle, but it wasn't far, either.

"I'll leave here in a half hour. I've gotta eat lunch and pack some things. Can you call Auntie Sarah at work and find out which hospital she's in? I'll call you for an update while I wait to cross the border, maybe in about a couple hours."

"Okay! I'll call Bev to get the Moms Prayer Group praying." My mom had a decades-long commitment to her stalwart moms prayer group, led by our dear family friend, "Auntie" Bev.

"Thanks, Mom! I love you."

"Love you, too!"

I hung up the telephone, wolfed down my beans and rice while my head spun as I quickly thought through logistics, and then grabbed my suitcase and threw my books into it. Trying to control my adrenalin rush, I stuffed my laptop, pens, pencils, paper, sticky notes, and pretty much everything else on my desk into my backpack, and headed out.

Four hours later, I dragged my suitcase down the shiny corridor of the cardiology ward of Swedish Hospital. Sunshine poured through the glass wall on one side, reflecting off the floor and onto the framed photographs hanging on the other side of the hallway. I hurried by the small black and white assemblages in the frames, but still stole a peek at them with fascination, remembering the many times Mom and Auntie Lillian recounted their service there as candy stripers, followed by their first jobs, in the hospital cafeteria. *A lot has changed in forty years*, I thought. Letting out a deep breath, I returned my gaze to the corridor, straight ahead. *A lot has changed in a day, too!*

"Hi, Grandma!" I said shyly, as I entered her hospital room.

Her eyes were open, gazing out the window, but she blinked when she heard me and she turned to see me. "Oh!" her voice was its usual high, sweet pitch, now weak and shaky, but undaunted as she focused on me and tried to sit up. "Well, hello! What are you doing here?"

"I came to visit you!" I said brightly, as I very consciously tried to sound as if I had simply come by for baos and tea and that wheeling my suitcase around her hospital bed to the other side of the room was the most normal thing in the world. I pushed my suitcase under the window seat and, grateful that my grandmother had a quiet, private room, settled into a chair and reached for her hand. "My mom called me and told me you're in the hospital. How are you feeling?"

"Oh, good. So good to see you!"

I smiled, though the parental Chinese way of expressing care arose in me. "My mom says you haven't been eating."

"Eh. I eat a little."

"Why aren't you eating, Grandma?"

"The food here. It doesn't taste good."

I wasn't sure if I believed that was her reason for not eating, but her statement was likely true. "Well. I actually brought you some food that I picked up on the way here. Good, clean, tasty food, because we both like that. It's organic and has kale, apricots, spring onions, and wild rice.... Want to try some?"

"Okay!" she said, and this time she shuffled the blankets around and managed to successfully sit up. Stuffing a pillow behind her back, I made a quick mental note of how lightweight she had become, and then I swung the overbed table to her and unpacked my grocery bag of to-go containers onto it. Soon I held up a spoonful of apricot kale rice.

"Too much!"

"Seriously? It's only a spoonful, Grandma!"

"Too much!" she repeated.

I reduced the spoonful to half a spoonful. "Okay, how's this?"

"Too much!"

"Still?"

"Yes."

Pause. Grandma wasn't giving me much room for negotiation. "How much then?"

"Half that."

I tapped out half of the half spoonful. "This is a quarter-spoonful. Don't tell me this is too much," I said with a wink.

"Okay," she said weakly.

"Okay?" I wanted to make sure she meant it.

"Okay," she said with resolution.

And that was the deal for the next half hour—Grandma ate quarter-spoonful by quarter-spoonful by the hand of her granddaughter. After that, we increased the amounts to half-spoonfuls, and soon after that, she was eating whole spoonfuls and feeding herself. When she was done eating for the time, I gauged her energy level. She was awake and alert, with no signs of wanting a nap. I scanned the near-empty hospital room for the upteenth time, searching for something interesting to talk about and to keep my grandma engaged, but its dark corners offered nothing on that front. So I sat again in the window seat and wrinkled my brow. When I was a child, my mom had told me the broad brushstrokes of some family stories . . . maybe Grandma could fill in some gaps . . .

"Hey, Grandma."

"Yeah?"

"Can you . . . tell me how you and Granddad met?"

Grandma leaned back into the pillows and the setting sun warmed her smiling face. "Ahh yes . . . I was a young woman from the countryside, you see . . . I had moved to the city for a nurse's education and lived with my uncle's family. The Reverend Paul Fong had just come back from America and was looking for a wife. He had a seminary music degree and played the violin, so while he was at church looking for a wife, we met because I was in the choir and he was guest-directing it . . . " Her breathing had relaxed nicely, and her mind was somewhere thousands of miles away, six decades ago. In such bliss, she had been thankfully oblivious to her surroundings up to that point. "What are you doing?"

I dismissively shook the diaphanous fabric in my hand. "Trying to shield you from getting the late afternoon sun in your eyes. But this window seat only has this thin stuff—"

"Leave it. I like it. The sun feels good."

I studied Grandma's face to make sure she wasn't simply trying to accommodate me, and then I let the ineffective gauze silently float back to the sides of the window seat as Grandma resettled into her reveries of Granddad. "One day I was on the bus going home to my uncle when the bus stopped and Paul appeared at the entrance. He came immediately to the seat next to me and sat down. I asked him, 'How are you?' He said, 'I can't sleep, I can't eat. All I can think about is you.' I said, 'You can have any girl you want! Everyone knows that you are the most eligible bachelor in our community. You have an education, you serve in the church, you swim and play tennis and write beautiful Chinese calligraphy. Why do you want to be with me? I'm an orphan from the countryside. I barely have any money working as a nurse at the refugee hospital. If you want to marry me, you must come home with me to meet my uncle.' So he did. Well, you see, my uncle and aunt had told me that if ever a man wanted to court me, I must bring him home for them to meet. So I did. Well, were they so surprised!"

"I'm sure they were!" I was beginning to see how my grandmother's penchant for being a straight talker went far back.

"The Second Sino-Japanese War happened in those days. We did not have much time before the ships would stop sailing. At Paul's request, the pastor of our church and his wife took me aside and asked me three questions. They asked me if I wanted to marry Paul. I said yes. They asked me if I was ready to marry a future reverend, and I said yes. They asked me if I was ready to go to America. I had never seen America. I had never been out of China when I was young! But I said yes."

"I remember my mom telling me something about this. There was a newspaper article about you and Granddad shortly after you arrived in Seattle. . . . Something about meeting on a Tuesday and marrying the next Friday. . . . Mom said you two left China on the last boat that made it across the ocean safely."

"The boat before us had to turn around. The boat after us got bombed."

"My goodness. So what was it like for you when you first arrived in America—"

"—Well, I see you have a visitor!" proclaimed a cheery voice as a tall nurse stepped into the room to check on my grandma. "Mrs. Fong, would you like a dinner tray?"

"Yes!" said Grandma brightly.

"Alrightie, I'll bring that to you."

The nurse disappeared, and there was a gentle moment of silence between me and Grandma. I was surprised, but pleased that her appetite had apparently recovered so well. A few seconds later, the nurse returned with the dinner tray and swiftly slid it onto the overbed table.

"Thank you!" said my grandma brightly.

"You're welcome! Enjoy, Mrs. Fong!" and the nurse whirled out.

"Here," Grandma mumbled, gesturing at the dinner tray. "You eat."

"What?"

"I got it for you. You need to eat."

"Nah, I can get food elsewhere. You need to eat more than I do. . . . How 'bout this milk? Milk is good for strong bones. When my dad was alive, he made sure my brother and I drank milk three times a day."

"I can't have milk. I'm lactose intolerant."

"Okay, umm . . . How about this Swiss Miss pudding? I remember when my family would visit you in Seattle and we would take the ferry to Kingston—I always got a little Swiss Miss pudding cup from the ferry cafeteria. It was a highlight of the trip! Want to try some?"

"What flavor is it?"

"This one is . . ." I quickly checked the flavor and also the ingredients list. Uh oh. It would be a risk. "'Chocolate Cream Pie.'"

"Okay."

"Okay?" I faltered.

Grandma reached up for the pudding cup. "I'll take it."

Just as I was about to launch into an explanation of the pudding's lactose-laden ingredients, we heard footsteps and I spun around, grateful for the distraction. "Auntie Sarah!"

"Hello!" sang Auntie Sarah. "I came straight here as soon as work got out. Mary Katherine, your Mom called and let me know you were coming. Is there anything you need?"

"Just a toothbrush. I forgot mine."

"We've got plenty back at the house."

"Oh, I'll be staying here tonight, with Grandma."

"You can't do that. There's nowhere for you to sleep."

"The nurse has already agreed to bring a cot for me when it's nighttime."

"There's all sorts of noises and activity that happen in the hospital. You should sleep at our place."

"My mom's prayer group is praying. I'll be fine."

"I'm glad they're praying, but prayer doesn't always work that way."

"I'll be fine. I can handle it." When it came down to it, my reasoning was simple: Grandma had to live with sleeping in the hospital, so I was certain that I could figure out how to do that as well.

Auntie Sarah acquiesced and tried another tactic. "I'm sure you can, but Grandma will sleep better if you're not here. She has more energy when people are around." I paused to consider Auntie Sarah's point, which in Grandma's case made sense enough. Then I observed my beloved Grandma, who had to listen to my aunt and I speaking back and forth about her, as if she wasn't listening. She appeared small, and I realized that I needed to end that conversation immediately.

"All right, but I'm staying here until visiting hours are over, and then I'll come back in the morning to be with Grandma."

"We'll have your toothbrush ready when you arrive," Auntie Sarah responded. "Grandma, I'm going to find the doctor to get a report on how you're doing," and then she was gone.

I turned back to Grandma. "So when you arrived in America—"

"Yes!" Grandma was full of energy now. "I arrived in America. First the boat docked in Honolulu, which I enjoyed very much. It was like a mini honeymoon, and the only time I wasn't seasick for the voyage. But we also didn't know I was pregnant. Oh, so many adventures with your grandfather!"

There followed a wordless moment, during which my grandmother's face beamed with her remembrance of Granddad and the adventurous early days of their lives together. They were refugees narrowly escaping war and death; they were international travelers with the glow of America ahead; they were a young couple in love and about to have a baby.

"So is that why you went to seminary after Granddad died?"

"What you mean?"

"Is that why you went to seminary after Granddad died? I mean, not many people in their sixties do graduate studies or live in a dorm!"

"Eh, well, Paul was a strong leader. I could not do as well without him, but I could still continue the work God called us to do. Trinity Lutheran gave me three scholarships! For mature students who enrolled full-time."

"I'm sure Trinity Lutheran is very proud of you. And think of all the children for the past twenty-plus years now who have benefitted from having a grandmother figure in their lives. Early Childhood Education was a good fit for your degree."

"I got an A in Greek, too!"

"Then you did better than me. I skipped class too much to get an A."

Like a good Chinese grandparent, Grandma perked her head up towards me. "Why you skip class?!"

"I didn't need it. The textbook was so good that I realized I could just teach myself by reading it. I still showed up for quizzes and tests and got a decent grade."

Grandma's head was still two inches higher than normal.

"It's okay, Grandma, I got As in second-year Greek. I haven't skipped any of my seminary classes."

Grandma relaxed and somehow shrank back down to her usual size, then rested her head again on the pillow. "I had to take a semester of beginning Hebrew. I got an A in that, too."

I was genuinely impressed and was about to say so, but caught myself.

"Don't worry, Grandma. I didn't skip Hebrew."

Grandma and I continued our rapport with her memories for a couple more hours until a sudden melodic phrase of three tones rang out through the hospital's overhead paging system. A calm voice announced that visiting hours would be over soon.

I hopped off the window seat and tucked the thin hospital blanket over my grandma's shoulders. "Time to go to sleep, Grandma. Let's pray before I go."

"Yes."

Holding her hand, I said a simple prayer. Grandma joined me as I said "Amen," and I opened my eyes. Her head was still bowed and her hand was still gripping mine. Her feeble voice continued praying, and though I could not make out all her words through the mumbling and muffling of things, I understood that now she was praying for me, thanking God that I had come and thanking God simply for me. Grandma prayed for safe travel for me to Auntie Sarah and Uncle Peter's home, and she asked God to bless me very, very much for what I had given her that day. I missed hearing her say "Amen," but at some point the room became very quiet and I wasn't sure if she had fallen asleep or was simply finished praying.

"Amen," I said.

"Amen," said Grandma, and then she released my hand.

I wanted to whisper, to honor the sense of sacred in the soundscape, but I knew visiting hours were nearly done and I had a practical task to do for Grandma. "Grandma, this light—do you want me to shut it off?" I motioned towards the dull, pale blue glow emanating from a fluorescent bulb at the head of her hospital bed.

"Yes, please." Her voice sounded childlike as she managed to snuggle into the simple linens.

I turned the hospital bed lamp off, but plenty of light still flooded through the window into the room. Cool and clear as crystal, peaceful and comforting as the bedding I wished my Grandma had that night, the full moon's gleam was pouring full-strength through my Grandma's hospital window—when she needed to sleep! I reached for the gauzy curtain with a huff and muttered to myself, "I don't know why hospitals wouldn't have thicker curtains . . ."

"What are you doing?"

"I'm trying to darken the room for you, but this curtain is not helping!"

"No, I like the moon."

"*That* moon? It is very bright tonight!"

"Leave it. I like it that way."

"Okay, Grandma. I love you." I kissed her cheek good-night.

"Thank you. Love you."

Over the course of the next few days, we repeated this pattern: I would arrive in the morning, feed or eat with Grandma, ask Grandma questions about her, Granddad, and family history, banter a bit with Grandma about my own life, welcome visitors who came in increasing numbers as word got out that Grandma was in the hospital, listen and talk more with Grandma until she needed to sleep or visiting hours finished, say a short prayer with Grandma to close the day, and head to Uncle Peter and Auntie Sarah's home to sleep. Meanwhile, Grandma recovered enough strength that the doctors thought she stood a reasonable enough chance of surviving a pacemaker implantation.

I pulled out my cellphone and spoke quietly into it. Grandma was snoring luxuriantly as I sat in the window seat, talking to my mom and with my back to a very persistent moon spilling a pool of luminescence over me.

"So you haven't been staying overnight there, have you?" My kind mom was checking on her kid, as always.

"No, though I tried. Auntie Sarah wouldn't let me."

"Well my dear, it's not the Ahwahnee!" Mom had a penchant for recalling the one time we had walked through that legendary hotel in her favorite national park.

"No place is! But we figured Grandma would sleep better without company here, anyway. While I'm not totally sure that's true, she's definitely gotten better quickly," I assured my mom. "She has been sleeping well and eating well. Lots of energy, too."

"Thanks be to God! Well, I've got a sub for work next week and a plane ticket for this Friday. Bev or one of the other prayer group moms will pick me up right after work gets out and take me straight to the airport."

"That's very kind of them, but I think the doctors are hoping to do the pacemaker surgery before then—as in, tomorrow!"

"Do you think she'll make it?"

"She's got a 60 percent chance," I quoted the doctors confidently, then dropped my voice. "Auntie Sarah and Uncle Peter are more cautious about it, but I figure her chances of surviving are . . . better than the chances of not surviving . . . right?"

Crickets.

"I mean, it's either we try this or she just dies now," I continued. "I think it's worth the chance."

"I agree. We'll keep this in prayer, and I'll be there soon."

The next morning Grandma was wheeled in a hospital cot to the pre-surgical unit. I walked beside her the entire way and we chatted about the artwork on the walls and the patients we passed by as if we were strolling through a park. For Grandma, such appreciation of her environment was natural; for me, it was a deliberate tactic to divert her mind and nerves from focusing much on her operation ahead. When we arrived at Pre-Surgery, a nurse offered to set up a chair for me.

"You're welcome to stay and keep company with your grandmother," she said, already steering a chair towards me.

"Oh, I don't need one. I'll just stand here next to my Grandma's bed, so she can see me."

"Are you sure? It's going to be a few hours."

"Hours?"

"Yes. We'll have routine tests and preparation to do, and there's a lot of waiting in between all of that."

"Ah! I'll take a chair then!"

The nurse smiled. "Here, you can take two." Then she turned towards Grandma. "Mrs. Fong, would you like a warm blanket?"

"Oh yes, please!" said Grandma.

"Here you go. I'll tuck another one around your feet."

"Ohh, that's so nice."

I popped out of my chair and studied Grandma lounging in her hospital cot. "Are you comfortable Grandma?" The answer was obvious, but I was in disbelief.

"Ohh, yes."

"Do you want to take a nap now?"

"Hm, okay."

"I'll be right here."

One nap, a couple diagnostic tests, and three hours later, Grandma was sitting up on the side of her cot, dangling her feet over the edge and waiting sleepily.

"You okay, Grandma? You don't seem nervous."

"God knows, and God will provide."

"I think we've still got another hour before the procedure."

"Can you wash my feet?"

"What?"

"Can you wash my feet?"

"Now? I don't think they're going to see your feet."

"I want to make sure they're clean. Normally, at the seniors' home, there is someone we can hire to come cut our toenails every week or two. It's probably been three weeks now."

"Well . . . let me see first if I can find a nurse with a toenail clipper here." I didn't think it was possible, but I was out of luck. We were even given a small bottle of body wash, a warm bin of water, and a couple towels. I propped up Grandma's feet and assessed the work ahead. On the one hand, it would be a privilege to wash my Grandma's feet—a real-life, practical, and literal application of Jesus' command to wash one another's feet. Much better than the symbolic footwashing ceremonies we did in young adult fellowships, I thought. And to be fair, cleaning my Grandma's feet would not be difficult; they did not smell nor were they dirty. That said, I had never seen her feet closely before, and suddenly there was a set of precious, eighty-something-year-old toes right in front of my nose. I wasn't sure where to start, if I might break something.

"Grandma, does this hurt?" I asked, barely touching a crooked toe.

"No," Grandma replied, nonplussed and apparently oblivious to how gingerly I was handling her digits.

I gazed at her feet a moment longer, struck by the story they told—these were feet that had frolicked buoyantly through the fields in the countryside with her two sisters as young children; these were feet that had gone cold in the winters while she tried to fall asleep in the orphanage after Great-Grandma had suddenly died and Great-Grandpa tried to drown the pain in an alcohol addiction; they were feet that ran into the arms of a kind uncle and aunt for family connection as she grew as a teenager; they were feet that had scurried throughout a mission hospital as she was trained and then served refugees as a teenager; and they were feet that carried her over and over to her Bible before anything else at church and thus attracted the quiet, serious eye of a young reverend searching for his life companion. These were feet that fled one home country to gain another, as the global movements of people in wartime changed her from one who served refugees to being a refugee herself. Yet beyond the chaos of a world war, these were feet that encountered a crueler cold in the harsh winters of the Pacific Northwest when the coal ran out and the soles of their shoes had worn so thin that they replaced them with cardboard; they were feet that wearied with the years of poverty and five small mouths to feed while Granddad traveled on trains and horseback to tend to small churches needing a pastor; they were feet that hurried to an exhausted Granddad every time he came home; and they were feet that collapsed under her while she wept at his grave. In time and with determination, these were feet that took her to the local Lutheran seminary and solidly earning her MA degree in Early

Childhood Education to serve children overseas. And then Grandma's feet soared—literally, for after decades of raising a family in the States at the poverty level, she returned to Asia, this time by plane. As a translator and trainer for Child Evangelism Fellowship, Grandma's country count suddenly exploded from two to twenty. She scooted around Hong Kong on the back of a motorcycle (my mom nearly fainted when she received a photo of that, though she memorialized it above the fireplace); she rode on the back of an elephant in Thailand; she zipped along in hi-tech trains in Taiwan and Japan. Most of the time, however, Grandma relied on buses and her feet in Macau, where she was primarily stationed. In that respect, her life overseas was not that different from what it had been in Seattle. But in every other respect—especially the physical distance from family—she had been a world away. This was why Grandma came home to the States for two to three months every year. Sure, on paper there were supportive churches to visit and conferences and workshops to attend. But beyond her official work duties, Grandma focused on simply living among family and close friends—she still needed us, and we still needed her. And it just happened to be the case that she had heart failure while she was home on one of these mini-furloughs... which was why I was holding her feet.

"Eh, everything okay?"

"Oh!... Yes, Grandma.... I'm just... not sure which toe to start with."

"You'll do fine. You won't hurt me."

"I sure hope not..." Thankfully, Grandma was right.

The next morning, Grandma woke up.

"Oh! Hello, Grandma!" Auntie Sarah sang out sweetly, scurrying to Grandma's bedside instantaneously.

"Eh..." a groggy Grandma responded.

"Grandma, you had heart surgery," I explained, jumping off the window seat. "You have a pacemaker now. Don't know if it should feel any different."

A nurse popped his head into the room and announced that the doctor would be arriving soon. Did we think Mrs. Fong could handle sitting up in a chair?

"Yes!" Grandma answered for herself.

Dr. Sokolov appeared in the doorway just as we got Grandma situated over a comfortable chair. His thin frame made a beeline for her and helped support her hovering form as she slowly lowered herself into the chair.

Whizzing around to grab a small stool for himself, he then sat opposite her and, clutching the armrests of her chair, bent down to try to meet her sleepy eyeline.

"Christina Fong! How are you feeling today!"

"Eh . . . good," Grandma said quietly, instinctively resorting to the Asian habit of lowering her eyes as a show of respect.

While persisting in his efforts to make eye contact, Dr. Sokolov proclaimed: "Your heart surgery was a success! Mrs. Fong, you have nine lives!"

Auntie Sarah, myself, and the nurse laughed. Grandma's voice found unusual strength as she said, virtually to the floor, "Praise God!"

"Yes . . . yes. . . . Now, I understand that you do quite a lot of traveling . . . in Asia?"

"Yes."

"She's a missionary in Asia!" I volunteered, "She works with children and the poor."

"Is that right! You are a wonder, Mrs. Fong!" Dr. Sokolov gazed at her with big eyes and a wide grin for a couple moments, then sighed with the mien of a doctor not yet benumbed by the hard news that was a hazard of his occupation. "Unfortunately, I'm afraid you'll need to do less traveling now. But, you'll be able to spend more time at home, to enjoy your lovely children and grandchildren." Dr. Sokolov waved his hand towards Auntie Sarah and me. "Will that be okay, Mrs. Fong?"

"Yes," Grandma said quietly. "God knows best."

"Yes, Mrs. Fong, yes. . . . God does know best."

While Grandma spent one more night in the hospital to recover strength before returning to Uncle Peter and Auntie Sarah's home, Auntie Sarah and I rushed ahead to prepare the house for her. Noticing that I was struggling to stay awake on the drive home, Auntie Sarah ordered me to rest upon arrival. It was a very welcome order, and when I woke up, a gentle, small figure was near the foot of my bed, quietly burrowing things out of her petite teal suitcase.

"Mummy!"

"I'm here," Mom paused her refolding of a pair of slacks and smiled at me in only the way that a mother can, as if I was her greatest treasure (and indeed, my brother and I always were).

"For how long?"

"Two weeks."

"That long?"

"I want to make sure Grandma has help during the transition. There will be some big changes to get used to."

"Yeah . . . did you know the doctor said she can't travel so much anymore?"

Mom nodded her head. "It's going to be hard for her."

"Yeah . . . I'm glad you're here. You sure you've got this?"

"Yes, you can go back now to Vancouver and finish that paper!"

"You're sure?"

"Mary Katherine . . . I know you didn't work on it while you were here."

I heard myself let out a short breath. "I didn't even crack open a book this entire week. And I hauled that suitcase up and down the hospital corridor I don't know how many times! I'm glad I was here, but if I want to graduate soon, you're right—I should go now."

"I'll be fine. So go now, but leave quietly; Auntie Sarah is asleep."

I reached with my foot under an end table for my weathered, old sandals. "Okay! Love you, Mummy!" I kissed my mom's cheek, grabbed my suitcase and laptop, and headed out the door—back to Vancouver, to my last MDiv term paper, to a ThM thesis, and beyond.

2

Calgary

I was adjusting the cherry wood frame hanging on my freshly painted wall when there was a knock on my office door.

"Come in! . . . Dr. Patricia Frost—hello!"

"Dr. Hom! Welcome to St. Jerome College! Just wanted to see how the new office is working out for you."

"Well, let me first say that it's an honor to be back in Canada. Took me several years to get back here—because I needed to get this thing called a PhD—but now that I'm here, it's a blessing," I said with a courteous bow. "Now, as for this office itself . . . it's okay. I could use more sunlight, like in those exterior offices with windows, but I understand they come at a premium and, of course, the senior faculty deserve them."

Jovially, Patricia dismissed my concern with a wave of her hand. "Don't worry—I know you just arrived, but you'll get there sooner than you think. Your CV is longer than the rest of ours combined!"

I shrugged. "We've all got our strengths. That's why Old Testament professors need Theology professors across the hall from them," I said with a wink.

Dr. Frost laughed. "And you know, an exterior office is not all it seems cracked up to be."

"What do you mean?"

"In the fall, winter, and spring, the sun hardly shines here in Calgary. Those exterior offices get nothing but a great view of rain, snow, and gray. And they get cold faster than the interior offices."

"That is a good point! It explains why most of my colleagues across the hall are hardly present in their offices."

"An unfortunate consequence as we're all still figuring out the kinks of St. Jerome's new building and grounds. But hey, if you'd like an escape from the cold, the Spirituality prof is needing more participants to help with his educational research trip in Malta this spring, right after Graduation. The college will subsidize most expenses for faculty."

"That would be awesome, but my mom deserves some time with me back home in California. She's been traveling a lot to Seattle lately to help take care of my grandma, and I don't think it's going to let up soon."

"Sorry to hear about your mom and grandma. You're a good daughter."

"Meh. . . . Well, you know, I have an awesome mom and sweet grandma! Hey, speaking of building kinks, I borrowed a stud finder from maintenance, and this was the best place on the wall. What do you think?" I stepped back so Patricia could see my work.

"It's fantastic! I wish I had a Cambridge degree! . . . So that's what their diplomas look like . . . " She craned her neck to inspect the faux gold leaf.

"It is. But ah—I meant the frame. Is it still crooked?"

"Oh! Uh, no, it's good." Dr. Frost did a quick obligatory glance up and down the frame, then promptly returned to peering at the diploma. "Does that say '800 years'?"

"It does." I reached into a box on the shelves and pulled out a worn hoodie. "My doctoral alma mater is pretty ancient, and they like to remind us of it. Some of my colleagues even delayed graduating to be able to say that they crossed the Senate House on the 800th anniversary. Me?—I just got lucky." I shuffled the hoodie over my head and produced a bandana out of its kangaroo pocket, which I waved towards the celebrated diploma. "But! my grandma loves it. If this wasn't here, it would be in my grandma's retirement home apartment next to a very large photo of my granddad and his violin."

"Your grandma's right! If I had a PhD from Cambridge, I would put it in a nice frame and favorite place as well!—You heading out somewhere?"

"Yeah yeah, I've got street ministry with Bridge Street Church tonight. We hit the streets every Monday night, rain or shine. Or, bearing in mind the weather today, I guess you could say, rain or rain!" I tugged at the hem of my sweatshirt. "Like my hoodie? My alma mater might be old, but this thing actually looks old!"

Patricia was amused, but not distracted from noting: "That's great that you've settled into a church so quickly, even before the school year starts!"

"It's a non-negotiable for me," I responded to Patricia while I secured the bandana over my head. Clicking off the small desk lamp light, I grabbed my backpack and turned to my colleague. "So, have you heard of the Calgary Stampede?"

"Oh! Of course! There's not a soul in Calgary who doesn't know what the Stampede is." Dr. Frost then proceeded to explain to the uninitiated American standing before her: "Every summer the city takes over the fairgrounds for what you Americans might call a state fair, except that it's just for the Calgary area. It tends to major on Calgary's cowboy culture and native heritage. If you're into rodeo, you can't miss it. Are you going to the Stampede tonight?"

"I think so, though . . . is it free?"

"No. It's not cheap, either, unless perhaps if you're just walking around the agricultural grounds."

"Hm, so if you were really short on cash but wanted to be at the Stampede, you would hangout at the agricultural grounds?"

"If you were short on cash, you would hangout nowhere at the Stampede."

My gaze shifted to the mostly blank wall for a moment. "Well, tonight should be interesting."

Two hours later, I was a short distance away from the Stampede, walking on a grassy bank along the Elbow River with Gregory and Rayeesha. It was a fresh and sun-kissed early evening in July—the hint of an early Chinook had managed to push back the afternoon's heavy blanket of stormclouds, such that the rain stopped shortly before we arrived at the fairground parking lot. Not taking for granted the respite from the storm, we enjoyed the stroll, apart from the fact that Gregory was shouldering a rather large and bulky bag, which he had assured us was no problem for him to carry.

"Gregory, are you gonna tell us why you brought the extra luggage?" Rayeesha half-poked Gregory, as he paused to switch hands and shook out a wrist.

"Yeah! It's full of good clothing in case anyone we meet needs it. I like practical ministry," Gregory enthused.

"It's great that you thought of that, Gregory," I spoke up, "But everything we're doing tonight is practical . . . *very* practical."

"Oh right, right. Well, I don't know what I think about those 'healing types' like Jay—"

"—our team leader—" Rayeesha interrupted, giving Gregory a look from under her cowboy hat.

"Oh yeah, don't get me wrong, I love Jay. I'm floored that he volunteers every Monday, every week, no matter what to helping the unhomed. He and Janice are great physiotherapists serving all sorts of patients in the hospital and clinics. They're some of my favorite people. But this miraculous healing thing, that's Jay's thing. I'm staying away from it."

My eyes slowly widened, and then I suddenly spun around and punched Gregory in the shoulder. His sack responded, shifting down. "Child! Is that why you volunteered for my group?"

With a sly grin, Gregory swung his bag back up his shoulder with another shake of his wrist. "Let's just say, I'm not a healer type."

"I'm not, either. But just so you know, I'm also not against miraculous healing. I'm not saying God necessarily works that way—as a biblical studies prof, I can affirm that the Bible is clear that God works both supernaturally and naturally. But with that being true, we can't dis-count the supernatural possibility, right?"

Gregory nodded that he was listening, and his sack obediently stayed in place. I thought a moment and added, "I was skeptical, too, but I've seen some of these healings Jay's prayed for on the streets and it's been amazing. . . . There's quiet stuff like legs growing out a bit, but then there's crazy stuff, too. A few Mondays ago, we were in downtown Calgary and Jay prayed for a big, tough-looking man with an injury that included two or three slipped discs. We all heard some faint popping sounds, and the man started bending his back and shouting four-letter words. He was like, 'Oh my G—, how did you do that!' He kept thanking Jay and asked if he could give him a hug. That was fun—especially because the man who got healed was so much bigger than Jay."

I winked at Gregory and Rayeesha, who were familiar with Jay's compact physique, then continued. "Last week, Jay and Kev found some young people hanging out under a bridge. One had been in a fight and had a rib that had been knocked out of place a couple inches, and he let Jay pray for it though one of his friends was mocking Jay and another just watched, saying nothing. The guy actually felt his rib move back into place and they all freaked out! The girl who had been mocking Jay ran away, and the guy who had said nothing just stood there repeating, 'I can't believe it, I can't believe it. . . . ' Jay told them, 'You know your friend, and what you've just seen is not from me—it's a miracle from Jesus,' and he told them about Jesus. After that, they all wanted Bibles!"

"I was there, too. They not only wanted Bibles—they got Bibles!" Lifting a couple pocket Bibles out of her messenger bag, Rayeesha gave Gregory a thumbs up.

Gregory shook his head, jeopardizing the balance of his load. "Man, that's awesome, but I don't know. . . . Why would this be happening now? And like, why here? Why not in a village in Africa or China?"

"I don't know," I held back for a minute and stared ahead, half aware of a small gaggle of people lounging on the riverbank in the distance. "But I do know that God has been doing these things in other parts of the world as well. It's definitely not just here. My grandma's told me stories."

"Like what?"

"'Like what?'" I repeated. I let out a deep breath and noticed both Gregory and Rayeesha grinning with twinkles in their eyes. "Okay . . . so when my grandma was a nurse-in-training in China, back in the late 1930s, she was working at a hospital when there was a really big earthquake." I resumed walking, but at a slower pace. "Like, buildings were crumbling and the whole hospital had to be evacuated. She said that even animals had started to flee the city center a couple days before the earthquake hit. At the same time, a major defensive war had begun between China and Japan, so the police were on the frontlines for that and there were none around to help evacuate people. My grandma wanted to stay with one of her patients, a Christian missionary too weak to move so she had to stay behind. The missionary insisted my grandma run for safety and not worry about her. So my grandma fled to the evacuation site, but she happened to look up and see the missionary being carried in a chair through the air past her. And when my grandma arrived at the evacuation site, her missionary-patient was already there, sitting in the chair, waiting for her."

"Are you serious?"

"Yeah! My grandma is a really straight-talking person. She wouldn't make this stuff up." I added, "She told me that the missionary said it was an angel who carried her in the chair to safety."

"That's wild!"

CALGARY

Rayeesha, who had been mostly quiet through this conversation, asked, "Was she the only one in your family who experienced that sort of thing?"

"No. My guess is that a lot of faithful Christians in impossible circumstances experience God and his work in a special way. I don't know if everyone does, but it's not just a family thing."

"So who else in your family had this sort of thing happen?" Rayeesha pressed further, pushing Gregory and his bag to the side so she could walk beside me.

"My Grandauntie Marian on my granddad's side was persecuted for having gone to a Russian mission seminary in China. She was tortured by the government and went on the run until she escaped to the States. My grandma has never let us forget her."

"Wow. So how—"

"—While she was imprisoned, they beat her until they thought she was dead. Then they ordered her family to come take her body. Three days later she revived."

"Wait—what?" "Was she really dead or do you think they just thought she was dead?"

"I don't know for absolute sure, but it's pretty hard to fake being dead to people who have your body."

There was an acknowledging sideways head nod from Gregory, while Rayeesha conceded, "True."

"So while she was dead or supposedly dead for those three days, she had a vision of heaven and the LORD. It was very peaceful there, and she did not want to leave. God told her that she would go back, and she protested. Then He told her that she would go to America. As it turned out, at that time her sister Rachel was about to pass away in California, and on her deathbed Rachel made her husband promise to bring Marian safely to the States. I don't know how Granduncle Joe did it, but he did." I paused the narrative for a moment, peering up at the sunlight through the dense tree canopy we were walking under, Rayeesha and Gregory in reflective quietude with me and softly crunching the pebbly ground underneath our feet as we walked. I then continued, "Grandauntie kept a low profile after that, but sometimes she would guest speak in Chinese churches and share about these things. I'm sad to say I don't know any Chinese languages, but I recognized every time she sang the melodies that she had heard the angels sing in her vision of heaven. I don't know if it was symbolic or what it really sounds like up there."

"Wow! . . . Your grandaunt was a saint!" Gregory exclaimed.

"Thanks! Yeah . . . well, I like to think we all are if we're committed to Jesus as Lord. It might just look different."

"Don't expect me to rise from the dead after three days!"

Rayeesha and I laughed, unintentionally catching the attention of the riverside posse. I felt a squeeze on my forearm, and I barely made out Rayeesha's words as she held her hat to her head and sped away towards the group. "They're waving at us; let's go!"

Gregory was too encumbered by his cargo, and I by my shyness of strangers to run. But we smiled at each other, Gregory steadied his pack with a flick of his wrist, and we followed after Rayeesha.

"Well," commented Gregory, "I guess we're not being intrusive!"

About forty minutes later, I was comfortably seated on my jacket atop the damp turf of the riverbank. Rayeesha had given Bibles to everyone and was now going from person to person, listening well as folks shared about their lives, and helped them find passages in the Bible that spoke to their ups and downs. Gregory had impressed with twenty minutes of extemporaneous preaching on the grassy hillside and was in the midst of burrowing through his tremendously sized bag to offer each person an appropriate piece of clothing before returning to more preaching. As for me? My role was to hold a team cell phone and try to keep everyone safe. On this evening, safety wasn't a problem; our "hosts" were a genuinely welcoming and friendly group of First Nations people who had fallen on hard times and were simply enjoying a pleasant evening at a popular spot by the Elbow River. Random pieces of trash and a few beer cans littered about posed no issue for us, and I knew they weren't necessarily deposited there by our new friends. Out of habit, I scanned the grass for needles, and saw no evident danger. I glanced down again at the cell phone's latest message from Jay's group: *Leukemia patient awesome small crowd now so we might be awhile.* I fiddled around with a couple blades of grass, surveyed our environment again, and quietly said a prayer. Through the riverside trees, the summer evening sun was throwing tea-gold shafts of light that were tawnier than the leather highlights on Rayeesha's hat when I noticed a gentleman sitting in that light slightly apart from the rest of the group. His t-shirt had evidently once been white, and I could not tell if he was simply being quiet or if he was tired. The light shifted again, and I could see that he was holding his forearm while his hand was wrapped in a bandage. As soon as I laid eyes on that, I felt an unusual compassion for him.

I scrambled over to him. "What happened?"

"Oh, I hurt my hand. The thumb got knocked out of place, so they put a nail in it. They'll check it in a few days." The gentleman was mild-mannered and very humble as he described his injury, and there was no sense of anger or bitterness in him concerning it.

"Would it be okay if I prayed for it?"

"Sure."

So, I prayed a simple prayer for healing for his hand. In the name of the Father, Son, and Holy Spirit. Then I opened my eyes. And I asked, "Do you feel anything?"

He answered, very sincerely: "No. But thank you for praying."

I felt the blank expression on my face. "Excuse me a minute." Pulling the little cell phone out of my pocket, I walked over to the line of trees. "Hey, this is Mary," I spoke hurriedly into the phone as soon as it connected. "Sorry to bother you all while Jay is doing his thing, but I've got a case for you healers."

There was a long pause, and I feared I had called the wrong number.

An unfamiliar, soft-spoken voice eventually responded, "Uh, hi, Mary, this is Timothy. I'm Jay's friend, and I'm just here to learn from him."

"Ah. Well, hi, Timothy! Welcome, and sorry we didn't see you earlier."

"Yes, sorry I was running late. We drove in today from Eston—"

"—Oh my, that's not close . . . !"

"It's okay. Jay is the most effective healer I've ever observed in person, and I'm not really a healer myself, so I've been waiting for a chance to shadow Jay for a long time. We'll see what God does, but at this point I believe people can learn, including me."

"I believe that, too, Timothy, but apparently I myself haven't learned enough. We need Jay or one of the other healers over here."

"No no, he can't right now. Some young guy with a badly broken foot got prayed for by Jay, and we all saw the swelling go down! Jesus totally healed his foot! The guy had a cousin who made fun of Jay the whole way until the guy's foot started to shrink back to normal. The cousin's attitude totally turned around and he almost fell to his knees when he saw that. Turns out he has leukemia, and he's begged Jay to pray for him."

"Whoa! Now I understand your group's text update better."

"Yeah! So, we're kinda busy right now. But you can do it, Mary. Just pray for healing in Jesus' name and watch great things happen . . . !"

"Well, I've done that before, but maybe we just need some persistence. I'll try again if the gentleman would like it. Thanks for the encouragement." I ended the call and stood there for a few moments feeling the warm sunlight on my face and silently praying. I turned back to the group—Gregory had resumed preaching; Rayeesha was still making friends and flipping through Bibles. Our new friends were passing around a bag of nuts to share and offered us tastes out of their beer bottles, but Gregory politely declined for the three of us. I returned to the guy with the bandaged hand. I figured we had nothing to lose—we were both just hanging out there with time to spare.

"I'm sorry I forgot to introduce myself earlier. My name is Mary."

"That's okay. My name is Sosê."

"Pleased to meet you, Sosê! Would it be okay if we prayed again?"

"Sure," responded Sosê, still the epitome of graciousness and chill.

So I sat opposite Sosê, closed my eyes, and prayed again for healing for his hand. "Amen," I said. "Amen," affirmed Sosê. We opened our eyes, and I could think of nothing more to do but to ask him yet again, "Do you feel anything?"

I studied Sosê's countenance over the bandaged forearm that he was holding up, and his eyes were wide open. He was gawking at something straight ahead—in my direction—but not at me. I didn't understand until suddenly a bandaged thumb sprang up, extending and flexing itself in our line of vision. "I couldn't do that before!"

I was incredulous. "Really?"

Sosê was just as astonished. "No, I couldn't!"

"Wow! Praise God! Can we—pray again?"

"Sure!"

So I led us in praying for Sosê's injured hand yet again as he kept it propped up between us. We opened our eyes. Before I could ask Sosê if he felt anything—

—The bandaged hand rose with force as it clenched into a fist!

"Dude!! You're freaking me out!!" cried Sosê.

"Yeah—me, too!!" I replied, barely able to think.

Sosê tried not to panic, while my mind was spinning, reaching for what in the world to do next. The answer seemed too obvious and natural: "Let's pray again and thank God for this!"

"Yeah!"

So we prayed a fourth time, with great joy and gratitude to God, and Sosê closed it with a humble "Amen!"

"Wow, Sosê, thank you for letting me pray for your hand. Is it all good now?"

"I think so! Look at this," he said, gazing in wonder at his wiggling thumb. "The bit that my thumb can't do now is just because the nail is in there." With a small hunch of his shoulders as he directed his attention to me, Sosê then said, "Thank you for praying for me."

"Uh, you're welcome? Though, you know, I think it's more that I prayed *with* you. I couldn't do this alone. Either way, Jesus did the miracle!"

"Amen!"

Rayeesha, Gregory, and I approached the Stampede entrance in the fading light of evening. Jay, Timothy, and a couple other guys were at our meeting spot, a flagpole, and had apparently occupied themselves with praying for a teammate's leg that was on the slightly short side.

"Ooh, that feels weird!" said the big fellow as he sat on the flagpole's concrete base with his feet extended.

Jay, still kneeling on the ground and cradling his teammate's feet, raised his head as we drew near and asked us, "Did you see that?"

"It's too dark to see that level of detail!" I chided.

The guy stood up and rotated his back and waist. "Yeah, that's good.... That feels great!"

Ever the physiologist, Jay insisted, "Try some leg extensions or walking on it." While our teammate jogged up and down a nearby sidewalk trying out his newly lengthened leg, Jay turned to my little group, his face radiant with joy. "Hey, guys! How'd it go?"

"It was great!" Gregory piped up. "We met a group of First Nations people just hanging out on the riverbank, and they invited us to join them. Rayeesha made sure all of them got a Bible, and they put up with a lot of my preaching."

Rayeesha recovered from her giggles and added, "Gregory also surprised us all by bringing—"

"Gregory? Is that you?"

"Pastor Larry? What are you doing here?"

"I came to see Jay in action tonight. Didn't know you were going to be here! Miss seeing you in the hockey rink!" Pastor Larry let out a good-natured laugh.

"Ohhh, that's deep! That hits deep!" Gregory responded while he joined in Larry's mirth.

"What happened?" I asked, confused as much by their conversation as I had been by the events of the evening.

"I accidentally knocked Gregory with my hockey stick last month," explained Pastor Larry. "So Greg's been off the ice all season. We're barely holding our own in the church league without him."

"Yeah, well, that's what you get for whacking my wrist!" There was levity in Gregory's eyes, otherwise I would have wondered whether a fight would break out. I myself was trying not to get upset, but for a slightly different reason.

"Gregory, you have a broken wrist?!" I exclaimed. "And you carried that—"

"Well hey, can I pray for your wrist?" Jay enthused.

Everyone went silent. Leave it to Jay—with his ardent eyes, joy-saturated demeanor, and childlike faith, he could innocently take over an atmosphere before he knew it. That, and we all knew that when Jay offered to pray, he wasn't joking around. Gregory's hearty laughter suddenly dissipated, and he looked at his dear friend Larry as he responded to Jay. "Oh . . . well . . ."

"You've got nothing to lose," said Jay. "And hey, how 'bout if we all pray together for your wrist?"

Jay, Larry, Rayeesha, and I were all smiling at Gregory with hope and happy anticipation. For a moment, Gregory had clammed up like a frightened kitten, but as he surveyed our faces, he said without wavering, "Okay, you can pray."

Jay called out, "Hey guys! Timothy, can you get the rest of your group over here? We're going to see a broken wrist healed!"

"Hi, Timothy!" I addressed Jay's visitor. "Great to meet you in person. This is our teammate, Gregory. We're going to pray for his wrist right now."

"Cool!" said Timothy.

"Can everybody gather 'round Gregory and lay a gentle hand on his wrist?" Jay called out over our reunited group.

We circled around Gregory, and like spokes on a wheel, surrounded his injured wrist. Jay and Larry prayed aloud, and then our dense knot of prayerers quietly drew back from Gregory to give him some breathing room. We were like a flower opening, and at its center was Gregory, standing there dumbstruck with his mouth agape and his body arched over his wrist as he stared at it in the last amber glow of twilight.

Oh shoot, I thought, *We've broken his wrist! Too many hands put weight on it.*

"*Noo-oe way!!*" Gregory exploded, shaking his wrist violently and throwing his head back such that we all could see the huge grin that had overtaken his face. "*No-oe way!*"

"Gregory, don't shake it so hard! You'll damage it again!" I shouted.

"Nah, God healed that wrist. Nothin's gonna break it now," Timothy said calmly, but with a deep exuberance that even his quiet nature could not contain. He stepped towards Gregory and reached out to gently lay his outstretched fingers on the newly healed wrist. "Healing's not really my strength, and I gotta hit the road soon, but before I do that . . . "

Gregory, still gobsmacked and with his jaw dropped, went silent again and simply stared at Timothy, whose own gaze was directed—like both a zephyr and a hound—towards Gregory's wrist. As Timothy's fingers landed on that joint, he spoke in almost a whisper to Gregory: "You have compassion for the poor and a heart for justice. This moves you to act in practical ways. Your heart is pure in this, and it doesn't matter to you if anyone sees you or not when you do these things."

I couldn't tell whether Gregory was going to just stand there forever or cry. But I heard him whisper, "Yeah, that's me."

Timothy stepped back as Larry sprang over to Gregory and bear-hugged him. "What a night this has been for you, bro!"

"You're telling me!" Gregory managed to respond through his stupefaction.

I spun around and caught Timothy. "Whoa, man, what'd you just do?"

"I just asked Father God what He had to say about Gregory and his nature."

I paused for a moment, thinking hard. "Yeah, but—what you said—that was . . . spot on. That is Gregory. He doesn't . . . he doesn't tell most people that. But it seemed to really matter to him tonight. I know you're into learning from others, so may I ask: Did you learn how to do this from somewhere?"

"I've been a few places, the usual ones for this stuff. But ultimately, I just read the Bible, pray, and find people good people to learn from."

"Did you say there's usual places to learn this stuff?"

"Yeah. They're mostly in the States."

"I'm from the States. Any in California?"

"Yeah! I went to school at one in California for a year. The program was okay, but the best part was meeting other students who are on fire for God. I can tell you more about it sometime."

"Yeah yeah, please do. No rush, but good to know for future reference. Did you learn much there?"

"Not really. Saw some interesting and crazy things, but I didn't really learn more than what you all are learning alongside Jay."

"Interesting. Are you glad you went?"

"Yeah."

Jay's voice sang out over our conversations. "Hey everyone, it's been an amazing evening! God's showed up, feet have been healed, legs have grown out, back pain crushed, a wrist made new, and praise God a leukemia patient walked home today having been prayed for and feeling 'fire' circling around his body multiple times! The sun's gone down and it looks like rain might be on its way, so . . . lemme close us in prayer, and then we'll head back to the church parking lot in our carpools." We swiftly gathered into a team huddle, Jay briefly and joyously prayed, and we reunited with our carpools.

Gregory was our group's driver, and as he drove us through downtown Calgary clearly enjoying handling the steering wheel with the appendage that had been healed, he could not contain his excitement.

"Praise God, what a night!" Gregory cheered ecstatically, nearly bouncing in his seat.

"Yes, I'm still taking it in," Rayeesha thoughtfully nodded from the passenger side.

"Gregory!" I hissed from the backseat as I peered at the red-gray sky rumbling over us. "Green light!"

Momentarily annoyed at the obligation to attend to driving, Gregory briefly watched the road as his car lurched forward to the next red light. "I still can't believe what that guy Timothy said! I don't even know him! He described me exactly—what I'm really about, what's most important to me." Gregory craned his neck around again to address me as he processed his amazement.

"Yeah, it's awesome!" I responded, watching small droplets of water collect on the window with increasing momentum.

"I mean, the guy's never met me! But he knew all this stuff about me, stuff that not even all my friends know. All he did was touch my wrist!"

"Yeah yeah, Gregory, all this is great, but could you please turn on your windshield wipers?"

I couldn't blame Gregory for his half-seconds of irritation with me, which were immediately drowned in his enthusiasm for what he had experienced earlier. Having quickly flicked on the windshield wipers, Gregory resumed his train-of-thought. "He said I have a compassion for the poor—that's why I brought the bag of good clothing. You and Rayeesha were the only ones who knew I did that. Can you believe it?!"

"Wow," I said, trying to squeeze forward over the car armrest so Gregory would stop turning around to speak to me. *At least the wipers are on*, I told myself.

"He said I have a heart for justice! He didn't know that I'm planning to go back to school to study law!"

"You whaaat?" "Say that again?!" Rayeesha was stunned, and I forgot about the rain.

Now having our full attention, Gregory announced again: "I'm going back to school to study law!"

"I—didn't—know that—" Rayeesha stammered.

"Neither did I!—" I chimed in, with a concerned look towards Rayeesha.

"How seriously are you thinking of going to law school, Gregory??"

"Very! I started filling out applications two weeks ago! I didn't tell anyone! Not even my mother!"

"Oh my . . . " Rayeesha was at a loss for words.

Gregory finally faced forward, settling into his seat and steering us through the storm. His face still beaming. "Praise God!! What a night!"

"Seriously," I piped up over the armrest, "I can't wait to tell my grandma all about this!"

I grabbed my organic burrito out of the microwave and stood over the lone table in my apartment. Carefully placing one stack of books onto another, then smacking a messy sheaf of papers atop it, I now had space for my burrito, my fruit-and-veg smoothie, and my cell phone. I pressed the button for the one number I had on speed dial.

"Hullo?" came the rough, phony low-pitched voice.

"Uh, Mom?"

"Oh, hi, Mary Katherine!" my mom nearly squealed, immediately switching back to her sweet tone.

"What's with the bass register?"

"Too many telemarketers."

"I see. You know, you could always offer to pray for them."

"I don't have that kind of time or patience. I'll pray for them when I meet with my moms group."

"Fair enough."

"So! To what do I owe this phone call?"

"I've been trying to catch Grandma for the past couple days, but no one's answered. I thought it might be just a poor connection because of the storm here, but I wanted to check that she's okay. Do you know anything about how she's doing?"

"My dear, last week your grandmother nearly burned down the retirement home."

"Excuse me?"

"Grandma nearly burned down the retirement home! She forgot to turn off the stovetop when her oatmeal was done. Again!"

I paused. "So—did anything actually catch fire?"

"Yes, though I think it was small and the fire alarm went off, so they caught it in time."

"Is Grandma okay?" I stabbed my burrito with a fork and readied to cut off a piece.

"We think so, though your Uncle Peter and Auntie Sarah have her staying at theirs for a couple weeks to make sure she's fit to live at the retirement community again."

I put my fork and knife down. There was an unhurried silence between my mom and me at that moment, during which words were not necessary. After some length, I finally said, feeling like I was just walking through the motions, "And if not?"

"If not, she will stay with Uncle Peter and Auntie Sarah for the time being. They have enough space in their house for her."

"I thought Uncle Peter had high blood pressure."

"He does."

"Doesn't he think Grandma talks too much? Didn't he tell her to sit down at Mae-Lun's graduation banquet because he thought Grandma was standing up too long to receive honor?" I was definitely past walking through the motions now.

Mom let out a long exhalation. "It will be okay for the time being."

"But didn't he tell her to stop saying hi to strangers and offering them help? Hasn't he reprimanded her in public for talking longer than he likes?"

"Mary Katherine, my brother has issues and my mother has issues. Nobody's perfect."

I quietly sighed, closed my eyes, and put my head in my hands. At some point, I heard my mom resume speaking.

"And I'm hoping over the next few months to get my house ready so Grandma can come live here eventually. With my physical therapy background, I can take care of her more easily than my brother can."

I knew it. "If Uncle Peter and Auntie Sarah can't handle taking care of Grandma, are you sure you can do it alone? . . . Maybe she should go to a nursing home."

"She can't afford a nursing home. . . . And Mary Katherine, she's my mother."

There was another noiseless moment, followed by another sigh. "Okay, how soon do you think this will all happen? How soon do you think she'll move to California?"

"Not for another year. I don't have the energy to go faster."

"Is it all right if I call Grandma at Uncle Peter's? I want to make sure she's okay."

"You can call her anytime. I'm sure she'd appreciate that."

I got my burrito out of the microwave for a second time and returned to the small, cleared space on my table.

Ring, ring! I heard the receiver get picked up and fumbled around for several seconds before a feeble and tinny voice answered.

"Eh, hello?"

"Hi, Grandma!"

"Ohhh! So nice of you to call!"

"My mom told me you are visiting Uncle Peter and Auntie Sarah, so I knew I could find you there. How are you feeling?"

"Eh, good. Sarah cooked steamed fish tonight! So good."

"Wow, that's pretty special. I'm just eating a burrito right now."

"When you come visit me, we will have steamed fish."

"Aw . . . well, Grandma, I'll get there. The school year will be starting soon, so I'll be locked in with teaching commitments until Christmas. But maybe I'll see you then or this summer."

"I hope so."

"Anything new happening at the retirement home?"

"No."

"No new events there?"

"No."

"Nothing unusual?"

"No."

I stared intensely into nowhere as I took a deep breath.

"Okay, well, I'm glad you get to spend some time with Auntie Sarah and Uncle Peter."

"How are you?"

"I'm good, Grandma . . . more than good. I did street ministry a couple nights ago. . . . God showed up. It was different than usual."

"Praise God."

"Yes, praise God—like really, praise God! Our head team leader is very gifted at healing, and God's been doing some incredible things through him on the streets, in the hospital, at church—a lot of places! So our team was sorta used to it—or at least used to watching healing and miracles happen. . . . But a couple nights ago was the first time that I got to be a part of God healing someone, like, directly part of healing someone. I barely knew what to do . . . and sometimes I didn't know what to do, but God still healed. . . . I've known in my head that these things are possible, but to be a part of it, experiencing it, is totally different!"

"Yes, I understand. Praise God!"

"Grandma, I could hardly sleep the other night, I was so excited! I'm usually not super surprised when God works through others like this, but if he'd work through someone like me, then, well, all bets are off—He can and apparently will work through anyone He wants to! I mean, I've always known that, but to experience it now . . . this changes everything! I'm still processing, but one of my teammates had an experience that was even more remarkable than mine, and his whole life is changing—new vocation, new location, and for now, probably even a new church to attend."

"Changes happen in life. Praise and thank God that He is in it with you."

I paused abruptly to consider my grandma's words, then continued. "Maybe someday I'll go to a short training or workshop at one of these 'supernatural-gifts churches' in North America. There's said to be at least one in California."

"California is good. It is nice and warm there. Close to your mother."

"I hear there is a better one in Chicago."

"Too far. You don't need it. God will teach you, like He has taught your team leader."

"Well, I am in Calgary, so either place is far. As for my team leader, he has learned from God through Scripture and experience, but he also believes he's learned some helpful things through some of the books being produced by these schools and churches."

"I will pray for you, for God to show you the best way to go."

"Thank you, Grandma."

"Where you are, is there a Chinatown, where you can get some steamed fish?"

"I don't think so, Grandma. It's more of a prairie culture out here. Chicken, beef . . . "

"Meh. You must come visit me. We have good fish."

"I will, Grandma. Hopefully it won't be too long before I can get to you. I do miss good fish."

3

Mosta

"Can you hear me? Patricia?" I grabbed the cage of the fan and yanked it away from me.

"Yes . . . yes, I can hear you. The connection is good. There's a little white noise in the background, but I can see and hear you."

"I apologize for the background noise. It's quite hot here and there's no A/C, so I've got the fan running. My mom also needed a nap, so you might hear her snoring behind me."

Dr. Patricia Frost was already kindly smiling at me on my laptop screen, but her smile widened further when she heard that.

"I'm really glad it worked out for May to accompany you on the research trip! It's always special when our parents can travel with us."

"Yeah, when my mom found out we'd be staying at an Ignatian prayer retreat center shortly before my grandma would be moving in with her, she figured she should take the opportunity to rest and have a little vacation while she could!"

"Well, Malta seems not so bad a place for that!"

"It ain't the Ahwahnee, but it's been perfect for her. Most of the time, we have been visiting and studying churches—four or five a day. And with the longstanding history of Christianity in Malta, even the local chapels put North American ecclesial architecture to shame! The food's been good, too—simple, but local and fresh. . . . Maybe too fresh, though: we were served a special dish of octopus the other day, and my mom was the only one who managed to eat any of it."

"Well, thank God May joined the group! I imagine you all needed her cultural sensitivity."

"We did. We needed her guts, too. I mean, it was a whole baby octopus on each plate—"

"Not easy for a North American, but perhaps you all will do better next time."

"No doubt my grandma could have eaten the whole thing. She loves seafood and has eaten everything imaginable," I continued. "But I don't think I inherited that part of her DNA."

"You've had squid before, right?"

I paused a beat, then looked Dr. Frost squarely in the eyes. "Did I mention that the baby octopi were still moving?"

Patricia could not suppress her groan as her eyes grew wider than the platters that our little Mediterranean octopi had been squiggling on.

"That's pretty much exactly how we felt, but we tried to be discreet," I said, giving my colleague a wink. "No doubt we were committing a cultural faux pas by not eating the live octopi, but the hosts knew we were international visitors, so one would think they would have taken that more into consideration."

Dr. Frost awkwardly cleared her throat and said with a bow of her head, "Fair enough!"

I smiled, albeit weakly, as my thoughts turned to the topic ahead. "Well, as interesting as it is, I did not request this online meeting to discuss the delicacies of local Maltese cuisine."

Patricia chuckled, lightly shaking off the shock effect of the live baby octopus dish. "What can I do for you today?"

I folded my hands in front of me on the small, wooden desk and exhaled. "I know this complicates things for the college, but I'm requesting a year off in order to return to California."

At that moment, I was certain it was much hotter that day in Mosta than in Calgary, but even through the lackluster Internet connection, I saw beads of sweat form on Dr. Frost's forehead and on the tip of her nose. "I don't expect to be paid during that time," I continued, "and of course the college is within full rights to not accept my request and just fire me. I wouldn't want that to happen, but I understand if the college decides to do that. The point for me is: I will be going back home for a year."

"All right . . . so . . . " Patricia struggled to recover her voice quickly, "does this have anything to do with the difficult dean that we had in the fall?"

"Not really. To be honest, it did get me thinking of leaving for a short time, but I think we worked things out enough. Nobody's perfect."

"Is it because you still believe Dr. Montclaire was harassed by that mature age student?"

"I am certain Dr. Montclaire was harassed by that mature age student, and I am still disappointed that our college did little to address that; she was right to leave. But that is actually not my reason for taking a year off."

"Are you leaving because some of your colleagues are leaving?"

"Some?" I scoffed incredulously. "You mean: many? Patricia, one-quarter of the faculty is not a small percent!"

Patricia sighed. "That's true."

"I really do just want to go back to California for a year."

"And what will you do in California?"

"I'm going to study the charismatic movement at some churches there."

"You could study the charismatic movement here in Calgary."

"I have. And it's taking me to California. That's where a lot of the teaching that's being produced about cultivating and stewarding supernatural gifts is coming from."

"Like what?"

"Books, videos, workshops . . . "

"Couldn't you read those books and videos here?"

"I've done that, too. There's not much left for me to do from a distance. And the thing is, I want to explore the culture itself, the community. What is it like to be in a community where everyone is pursuing supernatural giftings and activity? How much are people genuinely doing these things there? What's helpful and healthy and can be brought to other churches? The best way to do that—if not the only way—is to be there. I've found this is true with any exploration of a culture or people," I asserted, adding, "whether or not I can stomach what's on the plate in front of me."

Patricia was drawing random doodles on a piece of paper as she stared at her keyboard. "Would you—consider delaying exploring the California charismatic churches for a year? That would give me more lead time to find a sessional instructor."

"What do you need a sessional instructor for? I taught the entire Freshman class Old Testament survey this past year—a record number of students for any course at the college! You've got lead time, plus at least two full-time faculty still on staff who have taught the course before."

"Okay, okay, we gave you too big a load. No one's gonna want to pick it up. The truth is that we all knew admin was giving you a ridiculously big load, but we were desperate. Other faculty who had survived less knew there was a problem, but didn't want to fix it. Too messy. We hoped you'd do better than us."

Great. So they made me, the new kid on the block, the victim instead of taking responsibility themselves. I had no words that I cared to say aloud.

"Well," I eventually said, "that's honest."

"Is that why you're leaving?"

No point in going further down this road with Patricia. Likely admin will be forced to revise the faculty load issues if there is no junior faculty to dump it on, but I need to be elsewhere for awhile, anyway. "I'm not leaving. I'm taking a break and will be back in a year."

"Is that why you're taking a break for a year?" Patricia was not backing down.

I allowed a subtle side nod. "It got me thinking."

"So . . . you," continued Patricia, "you want to go back to California for a year . . ."

"Yes."

"To explore the charismatic movement?"

"Yes."

"How much does your grandmother come into play in all this?"

I did not move. So much for keeping family out of it. "She does."

"I'm not surprised," said Dr. Frost, kindly but with her eyes now seemingly incisively concentrated on the doodles on her paper. "I know you are very close to her."

"I hardly see her."

"You talk about her all the time."

"I am—probably closer to my grandma than most people are."

Dr. Frost raised her eyes, so I continued, "She's not getting any younger . . . and my mom thinks she'll probably die within the next year."

As if a gust of fresh air had blown into her lungs, Patricia now sat up and leaned back in her chair. "So that's it! I know there's a lot of issues here for the college to work on and reasons for you to take a break away, but this is really it."

"Well—," I reacted, then backed down, because Patricia was correct. "... yeah. They're all reasons to return to California. But you're right."

"Okay..."

Okay?

"... I understand."

I watched with steady eyes as the Theology professor formed her next thought.

"So, the honest truth is that no one at the college is going to want you to leave..."

"I appreciate being valued."

Patricia nodded as she continued, "And while the leadership of St. Jerome College encourages theological inquiry and exploration, I can guarantee you that admin will be scared if you leave to immerse yourself in the charismatic movement."

"Okay, wait—first of all, I'm not planning to immerse myself in it. But secondly—isn't the college into charismatic things?"

"Yeah, but not that kind of charismatic. We're 'charismatic lite.'"

I deflated with an audible expiration.

"Your colleagues would support you, I'm sure of it. But I can't say the same for admin."

"As usual."

"Well, yeah," Patricia conceded, tossing up her hands. She sighed and hung her head with a guilty expression on her face. "I'm sorry, but frankly speaking, they'll be afraid of what you'll become if you go."

I echoed her sigh. "I understand. I would think the same if I were in their shoes."

"But here's the other thing: your grandma."

"What about my grandma?"

"What if she survives beyond a year?"

With a sharp breath in, I started up. "Oh my gosh..." Hearing my voice fade as I processed this point, I was half aware that my colleague's visage was somewhere between grim and compassionate.

"Have you thought about that? If she lives longer than a year, would you want to take a second year off?"

"The doctors don't expect it, but it's possible she'll survive longer than a year..."

"And what if, by some miracle, your grandma lasts three years? Five years?"

"That is not going to happen. She's already in her nineties and has numerous health complications. I mean, I can't put it past God to keep her going for a couple years.... He seems to enjoy doing unusual things in her life."

"Right, so what would you do if she lives that long?"

My hands were clutched together in front of my face, and I rested my chin on them. "I would want to be there with her."

"You would want to be there with her?" Patricia checked.

"Yes—yes, I would.... Of course!"

It was quiet again, and I became aware of the whirring of the fan as it blew an old lace curtain away from the window and ripples of light washed over my snoring mom and me.

"Okay," Patricia's empathetic face was a melting pot of too many emotions.

The sunlight danced over my laptop, so I adjusted the screen. I wiped the sweat off the bridge of my nose, then sat up. "My friend, I think I'm going to need your help."

"Name it."

I took a deep breath. "I've never written a resignation letter before, so ... could you please show me how to do that?"

Patricia blinked quickly a couple times, then said with a weak smile: "Sure."

4

Drumheller

The hot Canadian prairie dust blew through the canyon, raced around the ringed and rugged hills, and pushed a tumbleweed past us as our straw hats were knocked to the ground. Rayeesha, Gregory, and I scrambled after our wind-tossed head gear while the ever-wise Lorna, who always wore a Tilley hat—moreover, with the wind cord secure—and Li'l Cal, who could not be bothered to wear anything on his head, kept our place in line.

"Whew! These badlands are no joke," said Rayeesha, still breathless. "I bet the dinosaurs just dried out here."

"I'm pretty sure the dinosaurs went extinct way before this place became a badlands," piped in Gregory, giving his rescued hat an extra thump onto his head. "But I wouldn't be surprised if humans dry out around here. From dust we came, and to dust we return!"

"Nahhh, no one's drying out here anytime soon," interjected Li'l Cal, taking an indulgent slurp from a fire-engine red coffee cup. "Timmy Horton's less than two miles away."

Rayeesha good-naturedly rolled her eyes at Caleb, who was a virtual younger brother to all of us. "Well, this production company did do a great job of setting up a passion play in a place that's, like, right between the city and the country."

"Yeah," I agreed. "I bet when I show my grandma photos of this, she won't believe that we were so close to a city."

"Speaking of photos," Lorna spoke up, "This actor who played Jesus is very popular and generous with his time with the fans! And did you notice all the people also trying to get selfies with Peter, Matthew, Mary Magdalene, and other disciples?—pretty much anyone with torn-fringe clothing and one of those cool wooden staffs! I think we might be standing here awhile."

"I'm okay with it!" Gregory boomed in an enthusiastically loud voice. "I really appreciate all that the actors and volunteers did to make this happen. I mean, that passion play blew me away! I'm so grateful," he gushed, before lowering his volume to add, "I cried twice."

"I cried, too," I acknowledged.

"Me, too," said Li'l Cal.

Lorna had a gentle smile on her face as she resumed her line of thinking. "Well, as the elder among you all, the point I was making is that I think we might be here awhile, so maybe we can take turns waiting in line and letting others get water and stop by the bathroom."

"Noo, you're young at heart, Lorna!" Rayeesha cried out.

"What? Elder where?" Gregory said almost simultaneously.

"John and I appreciate such love from you all," Lorna responded, her smile now wide and beaming, "but my point was—"

"Yeah yeah, Lorna, we get it—let's do it!" Li'l Cal enthused.

"We've all got cell phones," I pointed out.

Lorna took charge with all the sweetly commanding presence of a seasoned grandmother. "Okay, so why don't you two—" and she took Gregory and Rayeesha each by a shoulder and directed them towards the water station in the distance, "—restock your water and take a little break for twenty minutes? Then come back and we'll swap. If it seems like the line is moving faster than we expected, we'll call you."

She gave an enthusiastic Gregory and Rayeesha a wave and a smile as they headed towards the water station with their bottles. Then Lorna turned to me, looked me in the eye, and asked sotto voce, "Okay, so how are you doing? It was wonderful of you to gather us friends together for one last hurrah before you leave, but how are you feeling about leaving?"

Though I was accustomed to Lorna's motherly care for us all, the question caught me off guard. With not a small amount of effort, I moved my gaze away from a Lululemon-clad family at the front of the line who had further stalled the unofficial photo-opportunity queue by grabbing Jesus' wooden staff and rather animatedly insisting Jesus give them more poses with their toddler.

"I don't know.... I feel different things on different days. In general, though, I'm excited to be going to a church and program where I can observe their dynamics and learn how they do community life in what some call 'long-term revival.'" I paused, remembering my conversation with Patricia through my laptop in Malta. "I just wish St. Jerome was with me on this.... I mean, my colleagues are, and I like to think that St. Jerome himself is, but my bosses are not." I was quiet again, then let out a long, slow breath of air. "I was told that they would be afraid of what I'd become if I go.... I was sad and disappointed to hear that, but I understand—if I were in my bosses' shoes, I would probably think the same thing."

Lorna tossed her head and instantly emitted a sound that can only be described as an elegant guffaw. "I'd be worried about what you'd become if you *don't* go."

Until that point, I hadn't been aware that my view was of the dirt on my shoes. My head snapped up. I kicked my shoes clean, and I stared at Lorna, who, for a long moment, simply stood there gazing back at me with pride while I let her words sink in. "I've never thought of it that way. Thank you, Lorna."

"Thank *you* for going!"

"Yeah, well, I'm not there yet! And I'll definitely miss you guys and the folks in the young adult ministry."

"I'm sure. You'll be greatly missed, too.... I understand you were asked to go on staff with YA."

I shot narrowed eyes at Li'l Cal, who shoved his hands into his pockets and swung around to watch the screaming toddler riding gleefully on the shoulders of Jesus.

"I was. I would love to go on staff with the Young Adults team, and it would be such a great honor. I mean, really, everything in my life here in Calgary is currently wonderful! I'm especially excited about where God has taken a lot of the ministries this past year at church. But, I know the church will be fine without me. I know some people say that I have had a mantle, but if that is true, then that mantle will just stay here and someone else can take it up. I was actually a pretty reluctant leader, but the people at Bridge Street made it easy, and we have many, many capable people at Bridge Street. The church will be fine without me."

"So how much of that did your grandma tell you?" Our oddly likably snarky Caleb hollered over his shoulder.

"Maybe half."

"Family is a good reason to go home," Lorna said, now watching the athleisure parents with a twinkle in her eye as they finally extricated their child from Jesus' tresses and relinquished their hold on his staff.

"It is," I answered affirmatively and quickly—too quickly, I realized. After a moment of thought, I repeated, in a muted near-whisper, "It is."

Lorna gave me one of her big momma hugs. "We're gonna miss you so much!"

"Hey, so while we're talking about families," interrupted Li'l Cal, "the actor who played Jesus has been doing an impressive job with all these crazy kids."

"He would. Evan and his wife have two or three kids of their own."

"Who? You mean Jesus? You know Jesus?!" Joe exclaimed.

"I think so . . . !" I said with a wink.

"You know what I mean!"

"Yeah yeah. The Jesus actor and his wife were student colleagues of mine in seminary at Regent."

"That's cool."

"It's how I know he and the guy playing Peter got modest payment for their professional acting services. Everyone else is a volunteer."

"My goodness," remarked Lorna with raised eyebrows. "Can you imagine how much time everyone devoted to this production? That's quite a commitment—paid or not."

"Yeah. You need to really care about the Gospel and this production to give so much time and work to some of these roles."

"Yeah," mumbled Li'l Cal absentmindedly as he resumed people-watching. This time it was a group of teenagers surrounding Jesus and throwing shakas for a photo.

"In fact, some of these roles are quite thankless," I continued, now scanning the line of actors tarrying by the stagefront. My line of vision focused on a lone and quiet figure near the front of the stage, dressed in a heavy and richly adorned costume. Golden embroidery, fine silk, and a mass of chunky jewelry highlighted the many layers of his black damask robes and towering gold-embroidered headdress. His striking gray-white beard was immaculate, imbuing his appearance with nobility and an impression of authority. Yet, his finery did not seem to match his countenance. Without taking his eager and hopeful eyes off the people walking by, he had stepped back to create a more comfortable space for them to meet him, his mouth ajar as if ready to jump at the first opportunity to say *Hello!* For a split second, I was somehow reminded of my grandma.

"Yeah," Li'l Cal responded distractedly, leaning off to the side to keep an eye on the latest Jesus fan poses.

I was still watching the figure in the distance. No one had stopped to meet his friendly smile or join his space, and he struggled to not betray the pain of rejection. "If you play your role well, possibly no one would like you."

"What?" As if he suddenly woke up, Li'l Cal whirled around with a suspecting frown, and Lorna was clearly amused.

"Li'l Cal, I need you to help me take a picture."

"Yeah, but it's gonna be awhile before we get to Jesus."

"We'll get to my old colleague, but that's not who I'm talking about."

"What? Where are we going?"

"Just—come with me. Lorna, you're okay to keep our spot in line?"

"Of course!" said Lorna, unusually cheerfully and knowing exactly where I was headed.

"Who?"

"No one with a staff. Just follow me."

I tugged at Caleb's arm and proceeded to squeeze my way forward through the crowd. "Excuse me!—Sorry!—Not trying to get to Jesus—I mean, the actor!—" As we reached the front, Li'l Cal suddenly pulled back.

"Wha? Naah!"

"Li'l Cal? Where are you?"

"Why you want a picture with him?!"

"He did a great job! But he's misunderstood."

"Yeah, but he's—"

"—a volunteer actor. He completely donated his time to this play."

"Ehhhh . . ."

"C'mon, man, you don't have to be in the photo with him. But I do need you to take the picture."

Dragging his feet behind, Li'l Cal did not hide his glare of disgust toward the portly actor, who saw us approaching, and his face lit up with joy.

"Ah! *Hello!*" bellowed the old gentleman, throwing his arms wide open in welcome as the layers of ersatz gold necklaces on his chest jangled. His thick gray-white beard could not hide the huge grin on his face.

I ignored the terrified expression on Li'l Cal's face and enthusiastically returned "Hello!!" hoping both to give the actor the kindness he deserved and to distract from Li'l Cal's confused, mute state. "Great job playing Caiaphas!"

"Heh! Well, thank you!"

"Not everyone could pull that off! And I'm sure not many would want to try."

"Oh, well," said the Caiaphas actor bashfully, "we all just serve where we can."

"Do you always play Caiaphas?"

"Last year I was Annas, but the year before that I was Matthew!" he pointed out, with a good-natured chuckle.

I laughed with him. "Wow! That's versatility."

"Thank you! Well now, where are you two from?" he asked, kindly directing his attention to Li'l Cal.

Li'l Cal forced a toothy approximation of a smile and managed to answer, "Calgary."

"Ah yes, we have many people come to the play from Calgary. Also from Red Deer, Edmonton, and all the nearby towns." And on the conversation graciously rolled for several minutes, mostly between Caiaphas and me, while Li'l Cal continued to process the false dictotomy in his mind embodied in the actor standing in front of him.

Eventually, I pointed to the camera hanging on Li'l Cal's neck. "Would it be okay if we got a picture with you?"

"Oh yes! Absolutely!" enthused Caiaphas.

"I'll just—take the photo," Li'l Cal volunteered, holding up his camera.

Caiaphas and I gave Li'l Cal's camera big smiles, and I thanked the actor as profusely as if he were playing Matthew again. Then Li'l Cal and I headed back to the queue, his feet not dragging for an instant this time. I could hear his groan-like sigh as we reunited with Lorna, who had been rejoined by Rayeesha and Gregory.

"Hey guys!" Gregory greeted us, taking a swig of water from his bottle. "Where'd you go?"

"Ehhh—" Li'l Cal trailed off.

"Caiaphas," I explained brusquely.

"Sorry, what?"

"Long story. I'll tell you later."

"I think there's still enough time for you two to take a break and get some water, if you want," broke in Lorna.

"There's snacks for purchase at the gift shop," volunteered Rayeesha.

"I'm going!" cried Li'l Cal, running towards the patron services area.

"Wait for me!" I called after him, scattering dust clouds as my feet tried to catch up.

I put my water bottle on the cool concrete floor. As Li'l Cal perused the snack aisle, I crouched on the ground and sifted through sale baskets of dinosaur and Drumheller Passion Play keychains, hunting for small gifts for Mom and Grandma.

I think I'll just need to opt for one of those coffee table books, I thought to myself, scooting forward to make way for a customer shuffling through an umbrella stand behind me. *I wish I could bring back home to California something more distinctive of this play or region.*

I was inspecting a miniature, plastic, pea-soup green *Tyrannosaurus rex* keychain when I became aware of the delicate and sonorous clamor of wooden sticks knocking on each other. Then, there was a light thud behind me accompanied by a booming voice.

"Well! This should fit you just right!"

Still hunched over a basket of knick-knacks, I paused my rummaging, brow furrowed, and discreetly turned my head. I saw behind me a pair of wide, sandaled feet and a slender, cleanly whittled tree branch firmly planted on the ground. No closer to dispelling my increasing confusion, I slowly peeked above the umbrella stand.

"Hey! Caiaphas!" I cried out, jumping up.

"Hello!" said the portly fellow, now bedecked simply in a worn maroon t-shirt and khaki cargo shorts. He stamped the ground again with the walking stick he had unsheathed from the stand and nearly shouted, "I think this is just your size!"

I opened my mouth to say something. "Wha—uh . . . " was all that I achieved.

"This is for you!" said Caiaphas, extending the thin wooden pole toward me.

"I, uh . . . " I held the walking stick in my hands, taking a moment to appreciate its craftsmanship. It was a handsome specimen of naturally pale, cream-colored wood, finely sanded and boasting of several reddish-brown, diamond-shaped knots scattered along its remarkably even and fairly straight length. It felt good under my hand—smooth and cool, but with just the right amount of give and softness on the surface—and it was slender and light enough to easily carry between two fingers. All that did not compromise the fact that it was strong and solid and perfectly suited as a walking companion. Unadulterated by any gloss or coating, I thought it was the most wonderful piece of wood I had ever seen.

"It's—beautiful!" I suddenly found my voice and at the same time realized something. "Did you make this??"

"Yes!" declared Caiaphas, proudly smiling.

"It looks like the staffs used by Jesus and his disciples!"

"It is! I made them all for the play." Caiaphas gave the hand-carved staff a little shake. "It's for you."

Li'l Cal came over, his mouth agape, as Caiaphas pointed out to me a large, carved-out diamond shape on the staff. "See this?" Caiaphas effervesced, quite unaware of Li'l Cal approaching him. "It's perfect for your thumb."

"Oh—well—I . . . " I went ahead and checked the price on the tag. "Oh my gosh. It's beautiful, but I can't. Thank you, though—"

Caiaphas swiftly grabbed the tag on the staff and tore it off. "Yes, you can. It's yours!"

"Oh my gosh!"

Caiaphas gave the ground a resolute tap with the staff, as if to add another exclamation mark to his statements.

"Oh my gosh!" was all I could say; and then, humbled, "Well—thank you . . . ! My goodness . . . !"

A throat cleared near Caiaphas. We both peered behind him to see Li'l Cal stepping forward and reaching for the umbrella stand. His clammy hand grasped a very handsome specimen among Caiaphas' handmade walking sticks as he smiled nervously, but hopefully. "Do I get one, too?"

"Oh . . . " deflated Caiaphas, recognizing his reluctant fan. "That one is, ah, more expensive."

I dropped my head and tried not to groan at Li'l Cal. It wouldn't have mattered, anyway, since my young friend was paying no attention to me while his wide eyes fixed on Caiaphas. "Pleeeease??"

With his posture perfectly straight as he assessed the scrawny figure in front of him, Caiaphas gave a small huff. Li'l Cal was undeterred and impressively ready to grovel. "Pleeeease??" he begged again with a nervous smile.

"Well . . . " said Caiaphas, turning over the tag on the staff that Caleb clenched with now white knuckles. Caiaphas paused for a long spell, staring at the tag, while I began to worry that Li'l Cal might be desperate enough to reduce himself to collapsing at the feet of Caiaphas and weeping.

"Well . . . " repeated Caiaphas with a lighter tone in his voice and a corner of his mouth turned up ever-so-slightly. His hand slowly closed over the tag, and he tore it off! "It's a good day!"

"Yay! . . . " exclaimed Li'l Cal, though with a shade of reservation and cautiously studying Caiaphas' face. Had he really been forgiven?

Caiaphas turned up the other corner of his mouth and finally recovered a twinkle in his eye. "It's a good day," he gently and reassuringly repeated to Li'l Cal with a wink.

"*Yes!!*" exploded the penitent, thrusting both arms in the air and waving his new gift.

"Bro! Watch out for the beams!" I shouted.

Li'l Cal lowered his arms and smiled back at Caiaphas. "Thank you," he said quietly, putting his hand on his heart and making a deep obeisance.

Our t-shirt-and-cargo-shorts-sporting gifter stood tall and with utmost dignity before Li'l Cal. "You're welcome," he replied with an elegant nod.

Meanwhile, my thumb fingered the diamond-shaped hollow on my new staff. "What kind of wood is this? Did you make it from trees around here?"

"Diamond willow! Straight from the Red Deer River Valley!" he proclaimed, almost more to the fine stick than to me. "And this," he continued, giving Li'l Cal's staff a couple affectionate pats, "is poplar, also from the River Valley! I did give it a bit of stain and varnish. . . . Yours . . . " Caiaphas gestured back toward my diamond willow staff. "I did not," he said apologetically.

"Oh!—Oh my goodness, that is totally all right! I think it's better this way! Did you stain and varnish Jesus' and the disciples' staffs?"

"I did not. I should have, though. If you look closely, you'll see that Jesus' staff already has a crack growing near the bottom. Evan's been working overtime in this desert heat, and so has his staff!"

"Well then, I'm honored." I turned to face Caiaphas directly and followed Li'l Cal's example. "Thank you," I said with a small dip of my head.

Caiaphas smiled at both of us. "You're welcome," he said. "It's been a good day for us all!"

Li'l Cal danced ahead of me through a small cloud of badlands haze, futilely and gleefully perforating the dusty air with his poplar walking stick, which he swung this way and that in awkward, pure joy.

As I approached our friends, Gregory twisted his head away from his conversation with Li'l Cal and called out to me in disbelief, "Caiaphas gave you walking sticks??"

I glanced at Li'l Cal, who had the relieved and happy manner of a person who knew forgiveness. "It's a long story," I said, hoping Gregory wouldn't protest that I kept saying that. "But yeah. He's a very nice person. And obviously very generous."

"A good man!" piped in Li'l Cal.

"Well, this is quite a surprise!" said Lorna, who had been inspecting Caleb's walking stick. She returned his staff to him and then closed her fingers over my walking stick, examining it and turning it around to admire its diamond-shaped knots. "I don't know much about woodwork, but John does some. . . . I can tell these are fine pieces of craftsmanship." She ran her thumb over the hollow of the largest diamond. "This seems to be just your size."

I smiled. "That's what Caiaphas said."

"Do you think it will fit in your car when you and Rayeesha drive you back home to California?"

It wasn't a thinking question for me. "Oh yes, no problem! If it is a problem, I won't let it be," I said, looking towards Rayeesha, who nodded her support. I turned back to Lorna. "Do you think it means something?" I asked, searching her face for her honest thoughts.

"I'm not sure," Lorna answered frankly. She then smiled and handed back the staff to me. "At the very least, don't be fooled by appearances, and mercy and kindness are worth stepping out for."

A small huff came from Li'l Cal's direction.

I leaned on my new staff. "They are, indeed."

5

Sacramento I

I SPEED-WALKED DOWN THE white corridor, hoping that my choice of clashing styles wasn't drawing attention to me. My long black hair was held back by a bold banana-leaf green and Ochna yellow African bandana, while a faded, cream-colored Cath Kidston messenger bag covered in tiny, pale pink English roses bounced at my side. I wasn't earning style points, but few in this place would care about that, anyway.

3–40, 3–3-9, 3–3-7 . . . This was too familiar a scene now, and the only thing my eyes bothered to focus on were the numbers. 3–3-5, 3–3-3, 3–3-1 . . . *This is it.*

I paused for a moment in front of the open door frame to brace myself for whatever I might see, and then I swung myself through the entrance. *Grandma needs me, I'm sure.*

My eyes—or rather, my ears—found her immediately. Grandma was snoring indulgently, and her eyes were shut tightly. Though she was clearly asleep, her petite, round face did not appear relaxed. Her thinning eyebrow lines arched inward and her forehead was lightly wrinkled beyond its usual smile lines. The pride of her face—her normally smooth and ivory complexion, made porcelain-like by the one indulgence she afforded herself in her senior years, Queen Bee moisturizer and supplements—gleamed pale and almost ghostly in the blue-tinged glow of the hospital overhead lighting. At least her usual shock of thick, white hair—like the breeding plumage of the Snowy Egrets that we admired in the Sacramento wetlands—had evidently been brushed by an attentive nurse.

SACRAMENTO I

I tiptoed to her bedside, dropped my messenger bag on a chair, and sat down in another. Watching her face for signs of consciousness, I reached out a hand and laid it on her arm. Nothing. "Grandma," I whispered. No response. My fingers fluttered on her arm with gentle taps. "Grandma," I said, upping my volume just a notch. Her eyes opened.

"Ehh?" she said, still facing the ceiling.

"Hi, Grandma!"

Grandma turned to face me. "Ohh! So good to see you!"

"Thank you, Grandma. I am happy to see you, too, though . . . I'm sorry you are here in the hospital."

"Eh, not so bad."

"It's not?"

"No, the nurses are very nice. And they told me I can go home soon."

"Yes, my mom said you will be coming home tomorrow."

"Oh! Thank God!"

"Yes, thank God! But I didn't want to have to wait to see you until you are back at my mom's tomorrow."

"Thank you." Her voice was feeble, but grateful.

"Maybe I should let you go back to sleep now?"

"No," she said innocently.

"You sound tired. Your voice is weak."

"The air is dry here."

I hadn't noticed, but did a quick sniff. The air was thin and cold, tinged with the familiar, faint scent of hospital linen laundry soap and the earthy, bitter, floral aroma of a slightly wilted "Get Well Soon" bouquet nearby. "The air *is* dry. Okay, well, I just wanted to make sure I'm not bothering you."

"No . . . no . . . you are not bothering me." I wasn't certain I believed her, but seeing her struggle to sit up and appear more awake kept me from protesting. "Can you ask them to bring me some hot water?"

"I'm not sure they have really hot water to drink, like you have at home, but I can ask." I pressed the red square button behind her hospital bed, and a kind, rushed voice promised to present itself in a minute.

Meanwhile, Grandma continued, "I thought you were in Kenya."

"Close. I was in South Africa and got back a week ago. Less than two months before that, I was in Uganda, which is next to Kenya. But Uganda is a very different country from Kenya—the culture, political history, topography, economy . . . They share an alliance with other East African countries, but they are different countries."

"Is that where you got your hair scarf from? Uganda?"

I smiled. "I did get this bandana from Uganda, though I was told by the tailor that she got the fabric from Kenya. It's a scrap piece from a larger piece of fabric that the Ugandan tailor was sewing to make me a short-person's *kitenge*."

"What's that?"

"A *kitenge* is like the African version of a sarong."

"Ah so. It is beautiful fabric. The colors are so strong and shiny."

"It is." I tugged at the knot behind my head and held out with two hands the heavy folds of fabric to show to my grandma. She closed her fingers around it, then moved it to her lap, where she ran her hand over the folds.

"It's called a wax print. The colors are very vibrant, and there is a special technique that is used to get this 'cracked' effect in the print." I opened the folds and pointed to the reverse side of the fabric. "See how the colors are strong on both sides? That's how we know it is a good print."

"Wow . . . very pretty," said grandma, slowly folding the bandana back up and lifting it to her forehead.

"Ah—" and then I stopped myself. I had not intended to say goodbye to my bandana, but I should not have been surprised. I decided that then was not the time to argue over property boundaries and that I could simply snag my bandana back when Grandma returned to my mom's home. Right after I had helped secure the bandana to my grandma's head, an auxiliary volunteer stepped into the room. "What can I do for you, Mrs. Fong?" she politely asked.

"Eh, can I have some hot water?" asked Grandma.

"To drink," I added.

"Hm, well, I could give you some tea. Would that be all right?"

Grandma simply gave a single nod. In the voiceless seconds that followed, I realized that this was all she was going to communicate, and I knew she trusted me enough to be her mouthpiece at that time. Turning to the auxiliary volunteer, I said, "Yes, that would great. Thank you."

With a kind little bow, the volunteer exited to fetch some tea. I pivoted back to my grandma, whose eyes had closed, as if she had fallen asleep sitting up. Should I tiptoe out and let her rest now? Should I honor that she wanted me to stay and that she wanted to be awake? I decided to test the waters one more time, just to be sure.

"The South Africa service trip was okay," I continued quietly, "but Uganda was wonderful. Want to see some pictures?" I reached for the worn but sturdy canvas flap of my messenger bag.

"Wha?" Grandma immediately lifted her head and opened her eyes, springing to life like the motorcycle she used to ride around Hong Kong. I tried not to appear startled by the sudden change as she proceeded to shimmy herself higher against the starched white hospital pillows and eagerly replied, "Oh yes! That would be nice!"

"Okay! Well, so I've got over eighty photos from my trip. Do you want to see people, landscapes, landmarks, events—"

"Just show me all of it."

"Not sure we can do all of it—I don't want to make you fall asleep. It's a lot of photos!"

"Don't worry about me. Show me people, everything."

"Okay, I'll—"

Grandma raised a slow, shaky arm, as if reaching for something. "I need my glasses," she said with that weak voice again.

I turned in the direction she pointed in. "Ah!" and quickly opened the tiny drawer of the nightstand. I snatched Grandma's eyeglasses out of the drawer and fitted them on her. "How's that?"

She gave a small nod. "It's good. Thank you." With the sudden return of such weakness in her voice, I wondered if it was wise for me to continue, but I decided to try.

I cleared my throat. "Okay!" I spoke up with slightly forced cheerfulness, "I'll start with the people who hosted us in the first village we went to. They were so welcoming and kind to us. Before anything else, we headed out to meet the chief of the village, and children ran up to us as soon as we walked into the village. We only had two translators with us, so not all of the children's words to us could be translated during our walk, but the kids still found ways to communicate—they walked alongside us and put their hands in ours. Some of them were carrying those large, yellow plastic containers for water, and if children hadn't claimed both our hands, we would take our free hands and carry the containers for them."

"In some countryside I've been to, like Thailand and Cambodia, the children did that, too."

"Hm yes, they haven't lost their heart or sense of community, like us city-dwellers."

Grandma leaned forward. "What is the next picture?"

"That's the chief's home. In this region, people use several different kinds of materials to make buildings. The chief's home is relatively large and the walls are made of fired clay bricks. The local pastor and his family's new home is small but also has bricks. The oldest living person in the village, a sweet grandmother that we visited, has her own two-room home that the village is making for her with bricks right next to her family's house. The grandmother's house is not really on its own, but more like an extension of the family's home. In the meantime, they made a little room for her constructed of more traditional materials to keep cool and dry. You can see here in this photo that most of the other villagers live like that—in houses made of mud, sticks, and cow manure. They say that cow manure is great for sealing walls and floors and keeps the environment cool."

"I saw that in India, too. My! Small world!"

I smiled at my grandma. "Well, Grandma, not everyone has seen as much of the world as you have."

"Twenty-three countries!"

"That's a lot of global education!"

"Eh, but your daddy taught you to handle rough conditions. He taught you to camp."

"Just in campsites up and down the coast. Not that rough," I clarified. "Just along the way, whenever we journeyed to see you."

"Every year in Yosemite . . . "

"That was just in tent cabins. But we did go every year." Narrowing my eyes, I added, "My mom would have preferred the Ahwahnee, this super fancy hotel that Queen Elizabeth and President Kennedy once stayed in."

"Your mommy different. We were poor. She grew up with nothing. When you grow up like that, you dream more." Grandma was suddenly quiet for a moment, struggling to steady herself. I quickly grabbed a pillow from a nearby chair and stuffed it behind her back. "Thank you."

"Better not get you too excited."

"It's okay. . . . Show me more photos."

And so I continued. Forty-three minutes and two cups of tea after we had begun, I finished showing Grandma my photo album of Uganda. She was still awake, and in fact even more awake than before we started.

"You're not tired?"

"No. . . . Should I be?"

"Uh, not necessarily . . . " I trailed off, scanning the room for a display monitor to show me her vitals.

"Are you still in ministry school?"

"I was in ministry school years ago, Grandma. I'm at more of a church program that they call ministry school."

"Same thing."

"Well, sure." I figured I wasn't exactly lying regarding my opinion, but sparing my grandma a trivial argument when she certainly didn't need further stress. I caught sight of Grandma's vitals monitor in a corner of the room. Apparently, the volume had been turned off so she could sleep. Heart rate, oxygen level, body temperature—all were within range and steady, so my eyes steered back to my grandma in the hospital bed. "The program is actually almost over. What they call Graduation is this coming week."

"And then what? Are you going back?"

"No," I replied, without hesitation and shaking my hair—quite loose since my grandma had donned my bandana—about my face. "It was fine for two years, but that was enough for me. I think there are other places and people I need to be with," I said, gently patting her arm and smiling.

"Did you learn much there?"

I moved my hand to my chin and took a deep breath. Enough silence passed between us that I didn't need to say further words on the matter, but I did anyway. "I learned as much as people told me I would learn before I went there. I met some good people, and also some adventurous ones—I was even invited to go on a backpacking trip with a few folks through the southern part of Africa later this month."

"Is that camping?"

"Maybe sometimes. But—"

"You're going to Africa again!"

"Well—I mean—I might."

"When would you go?"

"If I go, it would be in two weeks' time. But I'm not sure I'm going."

"Okay."

I shook my head in disbelief. "No—Grandma, you're in the hospital."

For a few moments, all I heard were the whirrs and clicks of the machines in the room. Then, despite the frailty in her voice: "Your Mommy can take care of me."

I held my head in my hands. I was trying everything I could to not say the "H" word. "I'm not sure."

"You'll see."

I heard my involuntary sigh. Still hunched over, I beheld my grandmother while gripping the bedrails. I did not want Grandma to feel like she would be a burden, but I knew my mom would be challenged to care for Grandma in the hospice condition on her own. "My mom has a lot of commitments," I said, lamely.

"Eh, busy busy."

"She does a lot of good," I defended my mom.

"Yes." Grandma folded her hands on her chest and slid herself slowly down the pillow stack that had been propping up her back. I watched as her breathing eventually relaxed and she closed her eyes.

About a minute passed. "Grandma?"

Her eyes opened. "Eh?"

"Are you tired?"

"Yes."

"Do you want to take a nap now?"

"Yes."

"Okay. I'll head home to my mom's now, but we'll see you tomorrow, in the morning, and bring you home with us."

"Okay, thank you." Grandma closed her eyes again.

I put my hand on her folded hands and prayed for her. "Amen," I concluded the prayer. "Amen," echoed faintly the tired, weak voice of my grandma, eyes still closed. I kissed her cheek and noiselessly headed for the door.

I leaned forward and rested my forehead on the heel of my hand, as I sighed over the edge of the cozy little farmhouse table that my mom had set up in her dining room. Mom had said the table was pine, and she loved that it was round with drop-down leaves and painted charmingly white. Before Grandma came to live with Mom, the little round table sported one leaf up, and Mom was happily content to have a perfect semi-circle facing the sliding glass doors to her garden. She had a quiet pride and joy in gazing upon the velvety hues of her gladioli and the color pop effect of her tulips; on the hushed but steady growth of her Meyer lemons, pineapple guavas, rogue peaches, three varieties of blueberries, and biennial plums; on the abundance of her long beans, tomatoes, butter lettuce, green onions, dill, parsley, and lemon mint. It was like watching a thousand secrets unfold in the summer, and Mom's heart delighted in it. But for now and for the past two years, a shift had happened. Both leaves of the table were up and a second chair occupied the other side of the table, as well as a TV tray. Mom's cheery, home-sewn fabric tablecloths were folded away somewhere in the hallway closet and had been displaced by a transparent PVC cover. At that moment, as I sat there at the little dining room table, I was in a third chair gracing its circumference. Mummy never gave a hint of ill feeling that the view of her cherished, not-quite-as-tidy-as-before garden had become partially blocked, nor that the gentle and loving touches that she had added to her table had been necessarily swept away or ignored for the sake of practicality. As far as she was concerned, her new joy and mission in life were to serve her mother in the final days of her life. And so we sat there at the little round table in the dining room—the central hub for our family's life together—and discussed what changes needed to be made at home to support Grandma's hospice season.

"The hospital bed is already set up in her bedroom. I don't think she'll be walking around much now, so we can take most of the foam mat tiles out of her room," Mom said matter-of-factly, ever a physical therapist.

"Should we leave some along the side of her bed, where the portable loo and wheelchair are?" I asked, reaching into the bowl of fresh-picked blueberries Mom had placed on the table.

"I don't think it will matter for Grandma. Just keep them there if it will matter for you and Ben."

"I don't think my brother will mind, but we'll find out when he gets here in a couple weeks."

"What about you?"

"I'd take them out. It's easier to push the wheelchair around without them."

"Then Ben will feel the same way, at least about the wheelchair. We'll take them out."

"Maybe we should get a second portable ramp. For that inch-and-a-half drop out the back door."

"Yes. Grandma will want to get outside. I'll pick one up from the hardware store when I go grocery shopping—"

"Nah, I'll get it. I'll go grocery shopping, too. You'll be busy getting Grandma."

"You're right—thanks." Mom paused in the busyness for a reflective moment. "There's going to be a lot of changes for my mom. I hope she's going to be okay here."

"What do you mean? She's asked for years to be able to move here, and now she loves it here! There's no place she'd rather be."

Mom sighed. "Well, you know Mary Katherine, my mom *is* the extrovert of the family . . ." Mom's eyes swung in the direction of a photo on the mantlepiece. I had no doubt what she was referring to.

"If that's the case, I think Grandma would be unhappy anywhere. But I don't think that's the case. And Grandma is probably okay that her motorcycle riding days are over." Pause in thought. "Everything else—I don't know. But I'm pretty sure she'll be okay without motorcycle riding!"

We both looked towards the photo of Grandma sporting a helmet and sitting atop a shiny red motorcycle, and Mom quietly smiled. Then we were silent again. "You know, Mary Katherine, my mom is the person I've known longest in the world."

I had nothing worth saying. My mom's hands gripped and pressed together, and her face was taut. As her eyes looked pleadingly towards her garden, she pursed and bit her lips, and I vainly searched in my mind for a way to quell the rumble within her.

I finally said, lamely, "How long do you think she'll last?"

"She won't die while you're gone."

"Gone??" I quickly sat up, raising my head, and the table shifted ever-so-slightly.

"While you're in Africa," Mom clarified quietly.

"I'm not going to Africa. Not now, are you crazy? You need me here."

"Your brother and I can take care of Grandma."

"I want to be here when she dies!"

"She's not going to die while you're gone."

I wanted to protest, but I couldn't, because I knew it was true.

Mom continued. "Remember how Grandma came alive when you showed her your Uganda photos?"

"But they were just photos. I can stay home and show her more photos."

"They were more than that to her."

I exhaled a long breath and hung my head down. To be fair, they were more than that to me, too.

"Remember when Dr. Ching was dying?" Mom recalled her gracious and unassuming godfather, who had lived in Hawaii.

"I was wondering if you were going to mention him."

She recounted the familiar account aloud, as if to remind not only me, but herself and the walls and everything around us: "All the rest of his children were at his bedside, but he waited two days for me to arrive. When I got there and joined the others, he said, 'My last daughter has arrived!' and he said goodbye to us all. The day after I left, he passed on to glory."

We sat there in stillness for some moments. Eventually I checked, "You sure you and Ben will be okay taking care of Grandma without me here?"

"Until you get back, yes. You can take care of Grandma after that."

I managed a weak smile. "Okay. . . . If you guys are all right with it, I'll be all right with it."

The tension had somehow melted away from Mom, and she pushed herself up from the table as it emitted a thin squeak on the floor. "I'd better do some grocery shopping and get over to the hardware store so I'm not late to pick up my mom."

"No, I'm going to the grocery store and hardware store, remember? But how 'bout if you swing by the bookstore near the hospital and see if they have any maps of Africa . . . "

"If they do have any good maps of Africa, you want me to get it?"

"Yeah . . . I wanna show Grandma where I'm going."

"I'll get it."

6

Johannesburg, Gaborone, and the Mozambican–Northern Zimbabwean Border

MAY PUSHED THE WHEELCHAIR into a sunny patch of the patio, which thankfully was not difficult to find with the mid-morning sun streaming over the neighbors' orange trees and into her prolifically lush garden. She affectionately studied the occupant of the wheelchair and smoothed the pure, cream-colored hair. "Well, Mom, is this a nice spot?"

"Yes . . ." The old, wizened head slowly rose, regarded her daughter, rested her eyes momentarily on the garden, then continued in a sluggish voice, "Thank you."

"Still sleepy, huh, Mom?"

"A little."

"I'll bring your breakfast out here. That should help."

"Thank you."

May returned soon with a TV tray and three petite dishes—her "ice cream bowls"—holding a small serving of oatmeal, scrambled eggs, and half a grapefruit, as well as a glass of milk. "Would you like your toast now, too?"

Christina turned her head and squinted from one side of the TV tray to the other. "No, this is enough. Thank you." She lifted her hand and gestured toward May as she sought words. "Could—could you bring me my eyeglasses?"

"I'll go look for them," said May, stepping back into the house. Moments later, she reappeared with Christina's eyeglasses and a large, pink, leather-bound Bible. "Here are your glasses, Mom! I thought we could have some prayer time out here and pray for Mary Katherine."

"Yes . . . where is she?"

"It's Day 5, so I think she's on her last day in Johannesburg."

"I thought . . . it was someplace with an 'S.'"

"Sebokeng. Good memory, Mom! She is staying in Sebokeng, which is a township outside Johannesburg."

"How many people is she with?"

"I don't know. Mary said the number will be constantly changing as different people come and go with the group, and their hosts will vary from individuals to whole churches and orphanages."

"Is she planning to stay with the group the whole time?"

"I'm not sure. . . . She mentioned specific people and communities that she wanted to visit, and I'm not sure that's on everyone's itinerary."

Christina gazed straight ahead, and her voice seemed stronger: "She will be fine."

May turned a curious head toward her mother. "Why do you think so?"

"The people. Her hosts have been so hospitable. They picked them up from the airport, took them to the grocery store and the mall and some place where Desmond Tutu lived—"

"—Vilakazi Street in Soweto—"

"Yes. They cook for them. That Mama at the first house washed Mary's clothes. Someone else had a neighbor who brought them over to meet five generations of his family. The people are taking care of their visitors. Their houses are simple, but their hospitality is not."

A tiny white-and-pale-purple flower from May's long-bean planter floated across the garden while May's eyes traced its path. "I hope you are right."

"We have not been there, so we do not know. But we are praying. That prayer group of yours is praying. God will be with her. And God is with the people she plans to see." Christina paused and contemplated the garden again, this time herself noticing the little flower being lifted on the breeze. "I just wonder what she is doing right now."

* * *

I was still gingerly holding between two fingers a "*Nie-Blankes* Non-Whites" ticket when I noticed Paulus already proceeding into the other room. "Hey, Paulus!" I waved my ticket in the air. "Don't forget! Some of us aren't white!"

Paulus turned around in his corridor and returned in our direction with a sheepish smile. "Ah, I didn't notice you were so far behind me," he spoke to us through the many colorful and translucent hanging panels and fencing in the "White/Non-White" exhibit. We had been assigned random tickets, and Paulus followed his designation down the "White" corridor, while Thabiso and I had received "Non-White" and made our way down the other.

"It's okay. I'm really just behind because I'm reading everything I can in this exhibit. And I'm keeping Thabiso behind because I need him to explain a lot of these things to me," I added with a nod towards Thabiso. "There's so much here. I'm glad you said this was the best museum to see, though it is hard to see."

"Yes, we all know this is the best museum in Johannesburg. Even Thabiso knew without ever having been here before."

Thabiso partly suppressed a humored groan.

"I'm processing a lot," I told my friends. "I myself have never been through anything near this level of persecution and oppression. I had a blessed Grand Auntie who was imprisoned and tortured for her faith, and my grandparents suffered some hard, systemic prejudice, but it was not on the level of this."

"Like what?" asked Thabiso, in his soft-spoken, but very intelligent manner.

I gestured up at the "*Nie-Blankes*" and "*Blankes*" signs over the intentionally haphazard construction of the divided corridors. "Like this. The artificial division forced on communities, schools, trains, banks, buses, churches, hospitals, and clinics . . . the people you must associate with and, for good or ill, come to trust exclusively." We had been strolling slowly through the corridors as we talked, contemplating together the broken images of community resources that I had rattled off in my response to Thabiso, and now we reached a spacious room with a new exhibit. Three large standing blocks with narrative descriptions of Apartheid stood before us, and beyond them we could see the walls lined with lit display cases occupied by weathered, sundry objects. In the midst of all that was something that appeared to be a cross between a tank and a large camion.

THE MOZAMBICAN–NORTHERN ZIMBABWEAN BORDER

Paulus quietly paused his steps, while Thabiso silently ambled in and began reading the exhibit narration on the blocks. I started to follow Thabiso when Paulus caught my eye as he gestured to a space between the blocks.

"More than anything," he whispered, flinging his hand toward the vehicle, "I hate that thing!"

"Why?" My head was spinning, and I quickly put up a hand to pause action. "We—we don't have to go in there if you don't want to . . . " I kept my eyes glued on Paulus, and continued, "I'm okay to skip this part if you want. I'm sure there's a lot more to this museum that we can see instead."

"No, I'm okay with it."

"You sure?"

"Yeah."

"You sure, Paulus? I'm not kidding."

Paulus laughed at my concerned insistence and gave me a little push into the room. "Yes, I'll be fine!"

As we entered the room, I craned my neck to see around a narration block. The object of potential distress was a big, ugly, metal vehicle sitting corpulently in the middle of the room, with no case or rails to guard it and just a small pedestal sign near it, about the size of a postcard. I dropped my voice. "Okay, so . . . why do you hate it?"

"I was tortured in that thing."

"Omigosh! Paulus! How?"

"I was in a protest, and they just grabbed us off the street and threw us in. Then they beat us up in there. They threw us against the metal walls and hit us and kicked us and things I won't tell you. I hated it every time!"

I could barely speak. "You were in there more than once?"

"About ten times."

I noticed Thabiso kindly wandering over to us, so I spoke up. "Hey Thabiso! What have you been reading on the displays?"

"It's about Sharpeville and Sobukwe."

"Is that a person?"

"Sobukwe was a person. Sharpeville was a protest."

"Like Sebokeng!"

"Sort of. Sharpeville was twenty years earlier."

"I feel like I should be taking notes."

"Don't worry, we'll help you."

"Hey!" I hissed urgently and pointed towards Paulus, who had silently moved past the narration blocks and was approaching the old police vehicle—a torture chamber on wheels—on his own. Without a further word between us, Thabiso and I hurried to catch up with our brave friend, forming a small knot with Paulus leading the way. We kept our pace quick and our eyes straight ahead, with only me spying briefly the odious thing as we passed by. We turned away, muttering among ourselves the obvious: "No need to look at that thing—" "—No—" "—Not at all."

We reached the next exhibit and stopped abruptly at the threshold. Photos and maps filled the room, and thankfully no torture or execution devices. We caught our breaths and took our time there.

Thabiso came up alongside me and began to talk, thoughtfully and somehow without anger. "I was still in school when Apartheid ended, so I didn't go through what Paulus went through. But my parents' generation did, and they told me stories. Some of my relatives and neighbors are no longer here because of what happened to them. We live in Sebokeng because Apartheid created it, not because we wanted to. No one beats me up, but every day I am reminded of the differences. When I walk through a white neighborhood, people look at me suspiciously, sometimes they follow or bother me until I leave. If I go to a white store to find something, they won't give me service."

"That's horrible!" I cried, for Thabiso was one of the most gentle and self-sacrificing people I had ever met.

He raised his eyes to the displays on the museum walls—the narratives, the photos, the objects. "Why haven't I been here?" Thabiso's soft voice choked slightly, and then he cleared his throat. "I don't need to. What's in this place—I lived it."

We stood there for a long moment, and I bowed my head. Then the three of us walked on together.

* * *

"Mom, what are you doing with that stick?!" May had just entered the room with a piece of paper in her hand.

"It's Mary Katherine's stick. From Canada," Christina responded from her wheelchair, swinging the smoothed diamond willow branch in the air with both hands. "I like how it feels."

"Yes, I know. I remember you used it as a support staff. But no walking without a walker now. It's safest if I move you around in the wheelchair."

"I want to walk."

May paused, mid-step, dropped her shoulders, and stood with sudden sadness before her mother. Her eyes fluttered a couple blinks and she dipped her head down before Christina could notice. "I know, Mom, I know. I'm sorry it's hard." With one hand May lifted the stick out of her mother's hands and held it out horizontally to her. "You can still hold the staff. Just hold it this way, so you don't break my Chinese vases," she said with a wink.

"What is that?" Christina inquired, now noticing the paper that had been flapping about in her daughter's hand.

"It's an update from Mary. It just arrived, and I brought it out to read to you."

"Oh! Where is she?"

May drew in a long breath. "I'll need to show you on The Map."

"You just tell me where she is."

"Right now, Mary is on a bus headed to Gaborone."

"Where is that?"

"See? I'll show you on The Map."

"I thought she was in Cape Town."

"No more discussion until we go to The Map!" May gently took Mary's staff out of Christina's hands and positioned herself behind the wheelchair. She steered it down the hallway into the family room, where two large maps were taped together, laminated, and pinned to the wall. The two maps together boasted a view of the whole continent of Africa in a four-by-five-foot space, with black and red dry erase ink scrawled over it.

"Remember, the black line is the route the group was planning to take. The red line is the route Mary has been taking. Sometimes she is with the group; most of the time she is on her own."

"Why is she on her own?"

"She has friends and communities she already knows whom she wants to see."

"Is she with the group now?"

"She was with Paulus and Thabiso through a couple townships and a garbage dump community outside of East London. Paulus was preaching there with a team, and Mary taught Hebrew and Greek to the church leaders—remember, she wrote to us that she was going to do that? Well, the power went out that night, and Mary taught by the light of a kerosene lamp and two flashlights. She said her Xhosa translator was excellent and really the one who did the bulk of the teaching. After that, she visited friends in

Cape Town and went to Robben Island. And now . . . let's see . . . " May held up the email printout. She pointed to a large dot on the southwestern coast of South Africa and traced a fairly straight line from the dot towards a star on the east. "This is the train route that Mary took with the group—in economy class. It took about twenty-seven hours for them to get from Cape Town to Johannesburg. They got off right before Pretoria, where the star is. Then they got bus tickets to go to Gaborone, Botswana. Right before they got on the bus, Mary sent this email to let us know she is headed there. The bus ride is supposed to be about eight to nine hours long, depending on the border crossing."

"Not as long as train rides in China."

"Yes, I'm sure she remembers your stories."

Christina nodded. "What will she do in Botswana?"

"It's another transition point. From Gaborone, the group will get on another bus, to Victoria Falls."

Christina's wrinkled, small hand now reached out and joined her daughter's, tracing lines on The Map. She pointed to Zimbabwe. "I thought she wanted to go here . . . to meet church leaders who had been imprisoned for protecting Christians."

"She wanted to, but the group decided they didn't have time to stop there. She probably thinks it is safer for her to stay with the group, too."

Christina lowered her hand but continued to stare straight ahead at The Map. "Oh," was all she could say.

"You wanted her to go to Zimbabwe?"

"I taught her since she was of reading age about the martyrs of the Boxer Rebellion."

"That was in China."

"Zimbabwe has had its own kind of suffering."

May wasn't sure if her mother agreed with her or not, but thought it best to let the matter be. She tugged lightly at the handlebars of the wheelchair. "Well . . . we should pray for Mary either way. Anything can happen on this trip."

"Yes."

* * *

Something hadn't been feeling right. I sat down at a picnic table under a small tree and got out my small tablet device.

THE MOZAMBICAN–NORTHERN ZIMBABWEAN BORDER

Hi Rayeesha,

Thanks so much to you and Gregory for praying for me while I'm on this trip! How is UBC? And how is Gregory liking law school?

Right now I'm in Gaborone, Botswana, and believe it or not, I'm just sitting under a tree in the courtyard of a partially outdoor mall. I think part of it is still under construction, but what's here is quite nice and I'm definitely not roughing it. Please pray for me, though. There is no one left in the travel group whom I really know, and I've had this increasing sense of, well, dis-peace that's feeling like it's at a breaking point. I don't know if I'm describing it well, but I'm really praying and waiting on God for where I should be going next. It's such a strong sense that I'm ready to break from the group completely now and travel on my own for the remainder of the trip. They are really nice folks, I just think I might be heading in a different direction. Please, if you can pray, that would be so helpful!

Love you both,
Mary

I hit 'send' and took a bite out of a chicken sandwich. A minute later, the little tablet dinged.

Mary!

I forgot to shut off the sound on my computer, but I'm glad it woke me up. I'm praying now! Aww, I wish I was there with you. Except I need a job, etc., LOL.

Just promise me that you'll stay safe and won't travel alone. They're nice folks, right, so why not? If you do head off on your own, promise me you'll go back to South Africa where your friends are.

Rayeesha xoxo

I glanced up and smiled at a couple passersby, put my sandwich down, and felt my fingers fly as they drummed over the tiny attachable keyboard.

Hi hon!

So glad you left the sound off, but you can go back to bed now! Sorry, I didn't mean to wake you up! But I'm glad you prayed—I know your prayers make a difference!

I'll do my best to stay reasonably safe. The local people that we've met have been very kind and hospitable so far, so I'm not worried, but I do want to be wise. I'll seriously consider returning to SA, but you know, I have friends in Zimbabwe, too.

> *Seven years ago, I visited a theological school in Ndola, Zambia. I turned down the opportunity to see Victoria Falls so I would have more time to visit with teachers and students at the school. I'll never regret that decision, but let's just say I've been waiting a long time to see Victoria Falls! At the same time, there's now another theological school that would like a visit from me, but it's on another path, to Bulawayo, Zimbabwe. I've been told and have read remarkable things about the president of the school and his wife—he was imprisoned twice for rescuing thousands of people from forced displacements and leading churches in resisting abuses and human rights oppression by the government. Now they are leading recovery and pastoral education in their city. I would be so honored to meet them! But I would have to travel for sure by myself and would be too far from the travel group to be able to join them again. Not sure if I should risk it . . . well, the good LORD knows, but I do not! Please keep praying! Thank you and Gregory for being there. Going on a prayer walk now.*
>
> *Mary xo*

I hastily closed the keyboard over the mini tablet and resumed work on my sandwich, slowly chewing on it though I was now barely aware of the piquant tastes of fresh tomato, warm and tangy spices, and deep-fried chicken. I had about five hours until I was supposed to board the bus for Francistown and, ultimately, Victoria Falls. Crumpling up the empty paper sandwich wrapper, my eyes stared down the corridors of the ceilingless mall and its shiny white tile floor and glossy walls. I heard myself sigh, and I finally deposited the crushed ball of paper into a nearby trash can, tucked my unused napkin into a jeans pocket, and stood up from the picnic table with a toss of my backpack over my shoulder.

Glad for the warmth of the sun on that clear day, I began walking down a nearby mall passageway. About two dozen eye-catching shop signs—as colorful and sometimes intentionally kitsch as in an American mall—littered the sides of the corridor. *Should I stop by any of these?* I prayed, slightly hoping the answer was No and that I would be enjoying a long, leisurely walk around the premises. Then a simple sign with a green and white cross and the word "Clicks" on it stood out unusually to me. Could this be a pharmacy?

LORD, You know I've never been to a Clicks. What kind of store is it?

"You don't need to know that right now."

THE MOZAMBICAN-NORTHERN ZIMBABWEAN BORDER

I kept walking towards the Clicks. *Okay. . . . Do You want to tell me what we're going there for?* I was hoping He would take me from the Clicks to another, more interesting location.

His voice was strong. "Left leg pain."

Still I asked, *Am I hearing You correctly?*

His voice became too strong for me to intelligently question it. "Left leg pain."

All right—left leg pain it is! Hoping I wasn't crazy, I strode through the metal detectors at the Clicks entrance silently praying, *LORD, if by chance I'm hearing You incorrectly or this is a test of my obedience to You, please know that I'm willing to look like a fool for You!* For the brief moment that I had to reflect on what was happening, I wished that Rayeesha, Jay, and Gregory were there. They weren't, but I was reminded that God was, and He was all that I needed. I focused straight ahead and headed for the first two people that I saw—a young man with a clipboard and a middle-aged customer standing in the aisle in front of me, evidently having a discussion about the bottles of vitamins on the shelves. Out of respect for their time and because I wasn't sure if I was crazy, I decided to cut to the chase.

"Hi! By chance, do either of you have left leg pain? I know it might sound weird, but I'm just on a prayer walk and I felt like God was saying that there's someone in this Clicks who has left leg pain and needs prayer for it. I don't want money or anything from you. I'm a Christian, and I'd just like to pray for someone's left leg pain if they like."

The man with the clipboard brightened and said, "No!"

I deflated. For half a second.

"But," he continued, "I have right elbow pain. Could you pray for that?"

"Sure," I responded. "I don't see why not. Let's pray together!" And so we did.

"Thank you!" said the young man.

"Is it any better?"

"Eh," he tested it. "It's all right. You must come again and pray for us!"

"Really?"

"Yes!"

I brightened, then deflated again. The travel group was set to leave that evening for Victoria Falls.

"I can't. My travel group is leaving tonight for Zambia. But—is it okay if I keep praying through the store now?"

"Sure! Thank you!"

Somewhat in happy shock from the unexpectedly warm welcome to pray in the store, I began to weave my way through the aisles. To every person that I saw I basically said, "Hi, I know this might sound strange, but by chance do you have left leg pain?" And in every case but one (in which the customer walked away before I could say much, but that was perfectly fine—I did not want to invade anyone's privacy or force prayers on anyone), the answer was "No, but . . ." After praying thus for various pains and situations in Clicks customers' lives, I rounded past the last aisle-end display of cosmetic puffs with a sense of relief and gratitude. *Well, LORD, thank You for helping me take a risk for You! I came into this Clicks apprehensive about this, and now I feel like I know what I'm doing—I'm just doing my best to be obedient to You, whether or not the results are what I hoped for (it's still been worth it, because people have felt loved and blessed by You sending someone to pray for them even in a pharmacy store). Just two people left to offer prayer for in the store—may I be faithful!*

As I approached the two ladies, I noticed that they wore the same polo shirt uniform as had the young man with the clipboard. *Ah, staff. Well, this will be over more easily than I expected.* I said my now-familiar lines. "By chance, does either of you have left leg pain?"

They stared at me. *This may not be quite as easy as I expected.* Not knowing what else to do, I simply continued, "I'm a Christian, I don't want anything from you—no money, no nothing. I just really felt like God's telling me that there's someone in this store who has left leg pain."

Silence. The more petite of the staff ladies looked like she was trying to burn x-rays through me. At the same time, I caught sight of the clipboard man coming down the aisle towards us. Had he not been smiling more than ever, I would have thought I was in trouble.

I went on apologetically to the petite staff lady as he joined us, "But if none of you has left leg pain, that's okay and may it stay that way! I can hear wrongly. I—"

"—*I have left leg pain . . . !*" came the powerful voice from the petite lady, who otherwise did not move but continued to bore holes with her eyes toward me.

"Oh! Well, that's great! I mean, it's not." I shook my head in confusion. "But it is great—because the LORD revealed that to us, so He wants to heal it. Is it okay if we pray for your left leg pain?"

"Yes."

"Okay, could you put your hand on your left leg where the pain is?" I appealed to smiling clipboard man and the other staff lady: "How 'bout if we all pray together?"

Clipboard man nodded, and we all prayed for the petite lady's left leg pain to go.

"How's it feel?" I asked the petite lady.

"I felt heat."

"Is the pain still there?" I remembered that Jay had always had us ask, sometimes with the 0–10 scale.

"Mm . . . yes."

"That's okay—can we pray again?"

"Yes."

And so we persisted and I led us in a simple prayer again. "Left leg pain, I order you out of here and to the place that Jesus has prepared for you, in Jesus' name."

I looked up at the petite lady's face to ask her if the pain was still there. Instead, my attention was suddenly captured by an explosion of voices.

"Tomorrow!! You must be here tomorrow!" shouted the petite lady, pointing emphatically to the ground we were standing on.

"Yes, 8 a.m.!! Tomorrow!!" exclaimed the clipboard man.

"*Fire!!*" Suddenly my hand was grabbed by the other staff lady, who put it on her right shoulder.

"Ahh! What are you doing?" I cried, pulling my hand away.

"I have a bad rash there!"

"Okay, we'll pray for that! Calmly!" We paused temporarily to pray for her shoulder rash, then the pandemonium resumed.

"Tomorrow!!" repeated the clipboard man.

"Yes!!" shouted the petite lady.

"Why?" I asked, yet again confused.

"That's when we are all together. Right now, we are not all here. But tomorrow morning is our weekly staff meeting. Then you can pray for all of us."

"But you don't need me! It's Jesus who healed you. You can all do this. We all prayed together, right? The Holy Spirit is in each one of you," I said. "I'm just here to encourage."

"Please!" said the clipboard man.

"Yes! Please!" agreed the fire-shouting staff lady.

With a gesture toward the clipboard man, the petite lady said, "I was telling our assistant manager right before you came that I had been to the hospital this morning because of my left leg pain. The doctors could not find any explanation for it, so they sent me home and back to work."

"Is this true?" I asked in disbelief, though I knew by the beaming smile on the clipboard-bearing assistant manager's face that it was indeed true.

"Yes!" he was overjoyed to say. "Please, come back and pray for us all tomorrow morning."

I was humbled by their persistence and did not want them to beg. "I would be happy to consider it, but I'm traveling with other people and we are supposed to leave tonight for Zambia."

The smiles dropped with sadness.

"I—I would be honored to return tomorrow morning, but it would mean that I must travel alone after this. And I would need a place to stay."

"Ohh . . ." said the assistant manager, his tone dampened but also understanding. "But then, please, pray for us more before you leave tonight!"

"I will," I said with apologetic eyes. "I need to take care of something first, but I'll be back after that and will pray for you all again before I leave."

"Thank you," the assistant manager said, a small smile returning to his face. "You promise?"

"I promise. Yes, I'll be back soon!" I turned to go.

"You must!" called out the petite lady.

"I will! Soon!" I called back, waving as I headed toward the store entrance and, ultimately, the picnic table.

* * *

Christina sat calmly in her wheelchair at the little round table in the dining room while May sat opposite her and next to a petite, toned lady sporting a chic, short haircut and polo shirt dress. The visitor presented more the appearance of a tennis player than a hospice nurse and had perfect posture as she tapped at her laptop's keyboard.

"She's had less energy lately," said May quietly, hoping her mom could not hear her across the table. "She's only been able to tolerate one day a week at the Senior Community Center for activities. She sleeps all the next day." May paused for a glimpse at her mother, who was gazing toward the sunny garden and the late-summer tulips potted on the edge of the patio. They were persimmon orange, dragon fruit pink, eggplant violet, and bell pepper red, and they were a small, but precious joy to mother and daughter in the early summer season. "She asked me earlier today, 'Where's the baby that was here last night with some people?' but we have not had visitors recently. I'm thinking it's age-related dementia, but I'd be curious what you think, Stephanie."

The hospice nurse nodded and continued to click away at her laptop, taking notes. Her fingers rested for a moment as she studied Christina, still engrossed in the liveliness of their garden. "Yes, I can see her increasing dementia. There is lots of confusion for her." May nodded. "Is there any time of day when she seems more clear than at others?"

"When my son Ben gets home from work, my mom is usually alert for an hour, maybe two, and we all have dinner together. The first few hours she's awake in the morning are also pretty good.... My daughter has been backpacking Africa, so two or three times a day we'll review her journey on the map—" May nodded towards The Map on the wall "—and when my mom is more awake, I'll read her some of Mary's daily email letters to us."

"As a mother, that must be hard to have your daughter so far away in an unknown place." Stephanie had paused again her keyboard clicking and focused on May.

Without a moment's hesitation, May responded, "I entrust both my children to God. My late husband David and I had a difficult time starting a family, and I finally got pregnant with Mary when I gave it all—" May raised her eyes and a pointed finger upwards—"to Him."

A bright and quiet smile broke out on Stephanie's face.

"That," May continued, "and I threatened my husband with getting myself a Lhasa Apso if I didn't get pregnant soon. David hated dogs!"

The two women laughed, while Christina sat silently. Stephanie turned to her. "Well, Mrs. Fong, perhaps you should have a little dog!" she enthusiastically suggested. "They can be very attentive and stimulating."

"Oh no. Dogs are too much trouble. Dog needs to be fed, dog needs to be walked, dog needs to be cleaned. May is too busy taking care of me," Christina protested.

"I would love to have a little, white Lhasa Apso! But that is one thing my mom and husband had in common—neither of them liked dogs!"

With not a small amount of effort, the hospice nurse smothered her grin and cleared her throat. "Well, Mrs. Fong, we'll pass on the dog idea. But you do have two grandchildren who love you very much. Ben is here, and May said that Mary writes to you every day from Africa?"

"She tries to," Christina answered. "I pray for her every day while she's away in Africa."

"I see. . . . Mrs. Fong, you have a big heart!"

"Eh?"

"You're saving your energy for your grandchildren. You treasure having dinner with your family. And you're keeping track of your granddaughter as she's overseas."

"Yes! Today Mary is in Zambia."

There was a sudden *whoosh* from the tablet computer on the counter behind May and Stephanie. May instantly swung around in her chair to check the message.

"That's gotta be Mary," May said, picking up the tablet. "Huh. . . . Looks like her message got delayed. . . . And she's still in Botswana . . ." She glanced up apologetically at Stephanie, who was actually as excited as her clients—not necessarily because of the granddaughter's adventures, but because of the responses they were drawing out of Mrs. Fong.

May, deciding to respect Stephanie's time, put the tablet back on the counter. "I'll take a closer look at this later."

Christina nodded. "We need to pray for my granddaughter."

"Well," said Stephanie, smiling at Mrs. Fong while adding more notes to her laptop record, "this seems to have woken us up!"

* * *

I had lost track of how many times I had woven through the aisles of the Clicks store, praying for customers amongst the wares, pharmacists at their consultation windows in the back, and staff throughout. I had even walked a couple times along the queues of people waiting for the tills, praying for and with anyone who welcomed it.

As I stood at the front end of an aisle for a moment, praying silently and wondering where in the store I should go next, the security guard slowly approached me, his eyes as wide as saucers.

"You're not going, are you?"

"What? Oh no, just praying."

The security guard's face immediately relaxed into a smile. "Whew! Good!"

"I can't go yet, anyway—my stuff is in a locker in the staff room," I said with a chuckle.

"Ahh, good!"

I smiled back politely and headed down the aisle for the umpteenth time, noticing a mother and child ahead to pray for. But on the back burner of my mind, I began to wonder if the petite lady and the fire-shouting lady had insisted that I make myself and my things at home in the staff room not simply so I could move about the store unhampered. While I was certain my backpack was safe there, I also was growing certain that the kind staff were doing everything they could to extend my visit. Glancing down at my watch, I noticed I had been praying at Clicks for a total of three and a half hours. The Clicks staff did not know it, but I had to meet the travel group at the picnic table in about forty-five minutes. From there, we would walk the short distance together to the bus depot, promptly board the overnight bus for Victoria Falls, and within minutes be on the road to Zambia. This meant I only had about a half hour left in the store, and I needed to be strict with my time. After praying with the mother for her child (whom I discovered had twisted his ankle), I slowed my pace and, absorbed in thought, rounded the front end of another aisle. I nearly bumped into the petite lady.

"I'm going to the tills now," she told me. "It's getting busy in here!"

"I noticed! Why would there be this sudden rush of people shopping now?"

"It's the end of the workday. People stop by on their way home from work."

"Ah."

"You're not leaving now, are you?"

"Uh, no. . . . No, I'm not."

"Good!" said the petite lady with a pleased face as she resumed her hurried walk to the tills.

After that brief conversation, I realized that it might be wise to think intentionally about how to leave Clicks without causing a scene. I needed to retrieve my backpack from the staff room when no one was watching me, which might not be a problem since it was all hands on deck at the tills and in the pharmacy. I needed also to get past the security guard and through the entrance to the store without drawing attention to myself, which would be difficult, but—as I watched the dense lines of people snaking through the till queueing area and following the barriers in a stream exiting the store—I figured I just might be able to slip through if I could join a queue. Having already prayed through earlier lines of customers, my presence in a queue again, albeit not while doing prayer ministry, would not necessarily draw undue attention, especially as the staff was distracted as they tended to the many people shopping at that hour. I thought about the products in the store and decided to buy a couple nice yellow-ribbon-wrapped boxes of chocolates as gifts for future hosts on the trip; the fact that I would need my wallet to make the purchase would cover why I had my backpack with me. I observed at the staff working at the tills. Most of those I had gotten to know best were there, so I would get one last chance to see them. We would miss a proper goodbye, but I figured a quiet departure on my part would be best for all.

So, there I had it—a brilliant plan! I proceeded through the steps so successfully, it felt like clockwork: nervously but swiftly slip into the staff room and fetch my backpack; head to the aisle displaying gift packages and select two boxes of chocolates; get into a queue to pay. As the line progressed, I nodded discreetly at my friends behind the tills as they waved and smiled at me with knowing brows and expressions, assuming I was praying for customers yet again. Everything was going so perfectly according to plan that I was mentally patting myself on the back. All I had to do was pay for the presents and follow the queues out the exit, and the events of that day would be perfectly wrapped up like the yellow-ribboned boxes of chocolates I was carrying.

My queue led to the assistant manager's till, and he grinned jovially at me as I enthusiastically dropped the chocolate boxes on the counter and held out a small stack of wrinkled green, red, and brown paper.

"Did I get this right?" I queried the assistant manager, as he leafed through the Pula.

"Yes! Very good!"

"I owe you some coins, too," I acknowledged, fishing through my wallet pocket for exact change.

"Don't worry about it," he said, with a wave of his hand.

"No, no, I must."

In one small, deft sweep, the assistant manager pushed the drawer of the cash register closed. "Till's closed!" he said, with mirth in his eyes and a delighted shrug.

I opened my mouth, but did not know what to say.

And suddenly, I was shrouded in darkness!

Where was I? What just happened? There was a hushed split second, and then: *Gasp!* "Eeeeeee!!" "Aaaahhh!" Hearing the corporate inhalation and instinctive cries, I knew I wasn't imagining things. The exclamations disintegrated quickly into a confused mass of chatter that crescendoed in seconds as the night air was punctuated by alarm blasts throughout the mall. Soon, thin beams of emergency lights sprang on along the corridor of the mall, and their fluorescent glow streamed dimly through the Clicks glass wall. Automatically, everyone turned toward the source of the light— just in time to see the Clicks security guard close the entrance doors. I felt my face, which up to this point had been frozen in shock, virtually fall to the ground. My perfect plan had been squashed in the most unexpected, spectacular way! I was not only without a clue as to *how* to exit the Clicks— I was without a clue as to whether I should exit the Clicks *at all*. Everything about my plan had been destroyed, wiped away down to the foundations in a single, somehow perfectly timed power outage. And yet the one thing I knew was that the uncanny timing of the darkness and closing of the doors was beyond coincidence for me. The LORD was saying *Stop!*, but I did not know why or what to do next.

The crowd banter gradually died down as cell phone lights glimmered and flickered in the queues. The assistant manager had disappeared as soon as the power went out, but now he returned with a few portable emergency lights swinging from his hands. Staff set up the lights along the counter, and I watched as a trickle of people paid for their wares, followed the stanchions toward the entrance, and slipped out, one by one, through the glass doors that the security guard judiciously cracked open each time. *I don't know what's going on, LORD, but it really seems like You're saying Stop, so I'm not moving until You say so.* Glad there was still significant cover of darkness so people would not see my stunned and dazed face, I shuffled through the dark to a place where I could wait on God and listen. Ironically, that meant I carefully followed the queue through the dark toward the entrance and the light, but opted not to exit. Trying not to appear too awkward, I stood at an out-of-the-way spot along the glass wall, just two arm's lengths away from the metal detectors, and waited for the LORD to give me direction.

Well, LORD, here I am. I still don't know what's going on, but I know to wait. So I'm waiting. I'm not moving until You say so.

Silence.

I shifted my feet and put my backpack down. *I'm not moving . . . ! I'm waiting for You to show me what to do next.*

More silence.

Just waiting, no problem.

More customers walked by en route to the exit. I smiled and waved at a few.

I'm tempted to feel awkward about this, but I'm not quite there. I'm tempted to feel impatient in the waiting, but I'm not quite there. Yep, I'm . . . just . . . waiting. . . . Ain't gonna move until You say so!

Out of the corner of my eye, I saw a shadowy figure approach me. I peered through the darkness and saw that she wore the same sort of polo shirt that Clicks staff wore. *She doesn't strike me as familiar, but she has a Clicks uniform on. I thought I had prayed at least twice for every staff person here. I'm confused!*

The figure walked straight up to me, ignoring the queue set-up. She stood expectantly in front of me and waited. I still didn't recognize her, so I wasn't sure what to say, except: "Hello!"

"Hello!" responded the lady, who spoke with a broad gesture of her arms. "I want you to pray for me!"

Hm, must be someone I missed praying for earlier today. "Sure. You don't need me to pray, but I'll pray with you."

"Okay!"

"Is there anything in particular you would like me to pray about with you?"

"Whatever God leads you to pray!"

"Okay . . ." We bowed our heads and, though it was dark, I closed my eyes and listened. I was not hearing anything specific, so I prayed a fairly general prayer for the lady's relationship with God, her work, and her family relationships. "Amen," I concluded, and the lady followed with thanks to God and a humble "Amen." I opened my eyes and looked up through the dark at my latest conversation partner.

"Thank you!" she said, jubilantly. I respectfully gave a little bow in response. The mystery Clicks lady continued, tracing large, elegant circles in the air. "I want you to stay at my house!"

Did I hear her correctly?

As if she had read my thoughts, she repeated, "I want you to stay at my house!"

With effort, I voicelessly accomplished half a nod.

"*I* am the manager!"

For a split second, I thought I might faint. I still could not speak.

The darkness must have covered my social obtuseness in these moments, because the Clicks store manager, evidently unperturbed, continued,

"All day long, my people have been coming to me and telling me what has been going on. And I wanted to come out to see you, but as the manager, I have to stay in the back room where the security monitors and computers are."

More nodding from me.

"But when the power went out, the computers went out, so I no longer needed to stay in the back. Nothing worked, it was completely dark in there! So, I could lock up the room and come out to see you."

I still could not talk. All I could do was listen.

"So I want you to come to my home, we'll have dinner, and I want you to tell me more about these things, and to pray for my family. And then, in the morning, we will come back here at 8 a.m. for the weekly staff meeting, and you can pray for us all then!"

Having been reduced to speechless staring, I eventually heard myself take a deep breath and say, "Okay, wow. Yeah . . . um . . . " The manager stood before me politely, the epitome of good manners and hospitality, while I fumbled for thoughts and words in this avalanche of new information, along with everything else that had happened in the past fifteen, twenty minutes. "I—I would like to, but I'm traveling with a group, so I would need to check with them first that it's okay if I leave the group now."

Undeterred, she said, "Okay."

"I need to, um, go meet them—" I squinted at my watch in the faint light of the emergency beams "—in about ten minutes at the picnic table in the courtyard." I caught sight of the store manager's countenance, full of expectancy, patience, and unyielding focus. If ever in my life I've encountered someone who was listening well—before I met my husband—this was the moment. "I'm pretty sure they'll be okay with it, so I'll just go now and come back after I talk with them."

"Okay, I'll come with you!"

"Oh, I'll just come back. No need to drag you there—"

"—Wait for me! All I have to do is get my bag. I already locked up the back. If you can wait for fifteen minutes, we'll be through the last customers and I'll have the rest of the store locked up." She must have noticed the skeptical expression on my face, because she added, "Normally, I am here for another hour, hour and a half after closing time to finish emails and close the shop. But because of this power outage, I can go home early now. Just fifteen minutes!"

"I've got to make it ten, but you can join me at the picnic table."

"Okay, ten! Don't leave without me."

***

Twelve days later, May was intensely staring at the computer screen. She grabbed the mouse, then pounded into the keyboard. Snoring luxuriantly behind her was Christina, who had fallen asleep in her wheelchair. May clicked "send," and the accompanying *whoosh!* startled Christina awake.

"What you doing?" Christina's frail, thin voice asked.

"I needed to change one of Mary Katherine's flights for her. The internet doesn't work where she is staying in Zimbabwe."

"Will she stay in Africa longer?"

"No, she'll stay the full fifty days as planned, then come home. But she has a totally new itinerary now that she's travelling alone."

"This is much better. The local people have treated her so well. And she got to be on a chicken bus!"

"Well, Mom, Mary said a chicken bus is a bus that is so packed with people that it's like a bus packed with chickens! So there probably weren't many chickens on the bus that Mary took into Zimbabwe."

"She got to stay with the pastor and his wife who were persecuted for rescuing local church people losing their homes. She got to attend classes and guest teach at the theological college there. She visited an orphanage and took some orphans to see lions!"

"Yes, she's had a lot of special experiences in Bulawayo."

"Bula—?"

"—Zimbabwe."

"Ah so."

"God knows, it was good Mary stayed another day in Gaborone. I mean, Botswana."

"Yes."

"Who would've guessed a lady would faint in the Clicks store the next day while Mary was away eating lunch?"

"Mary was not happy that the staff did not pray for the lady who fainted until she returned."

"She was very upset. She doesn't want people making an idol of her or depending on her instead of going directly to God. Mary is just a person. You and I know that."

"If you see a person ministering for only an hour or two, you tend to think better of them because you don't see them every day."

May quickly suppressed a smile upon hearing her mother say this. In her missionary days, Christina had gained an admirable reputation as a speaker and teacher. But at home, with her strong will, "Mrs. Fong" had not always been the easiest person to discuss hard things with.

Christina's voice interrupted her thoughts. "Where will Mary go after Zimbabwe?"

"Mary plans to visit a lovely Christian couple active in Malawi's legal structure for a few days. They did their graduate degrees in England, which is how Mary knows 'em . . . " May's articulation trailed off as she turned to the flight schedule on the computer screen. She clicked the mouse a few times, then continued. "From there, Mary will *somehow* get to Johannesburg, where she'll take a flight to Pemba in Mozambique to spend a couple weeks at an orphanage. And then she'll come home."

"You're not sure how Mary will travel?"

"I don't know how she'll get to Johannesburg from Blantyre. She said something about taking a bus, but it's a thirty-three-hour journey through four countries."

"We will pray," said Christina.

"You're right, Mom. We must. I'll call Bev to update the Moms Prayer Group. The people Mary has met have been stunning. Wonderful! I just don't know if my kid knows what she's taken on, though. Travel is rough!"

"Your family went camping every year."

"That was tent cabins in Curry Village, in Yosemite. Or camping in state parks or national forests on the way to visit you. What Mary is doing is beyond American camping!"

"The locals will teach her. Mary respects them." Christina started to lower her head, as if nodding off, then suddenly raised it, remembering something. "Can you show me the photos again of Mary with the orphans in the lion park? In Zimbabwe?"

May's eyes, focused again on the computer screen, blinked a couple times, and she answered, "Sure, Mom. Just let me check this re-booking first."

* * *

I sat on a concrete block on the Zimbabwean side of the border with my passport in my hand. With not much else to do—and grateful for that—I examined again the large neon-yellow-and-tangerine-colored visa sticker with its stamps and scribbles. It had been a long process, but there was a familiarity to it now. Nonetheless, I owed a great part of the success of my border crossings to the community efforts of a wise bus driver, two Malawian passengers who had taken me under their wings, and a compassionate busload of fellow travelers who generously and altruistically held that if the one non-majority-African passenger on the bus did not make it through immigration or was delayed, they would all be delayed. This was a value on the part of the passengers that took me by surprise and, yet again, humbled me. I had begun the journey concerned about the risk of being left behind at a border, but soon realized that the people did not consider leaving anyone behind—this foreigner included—as a valid option. For this reason, the bus staff and passengers all prodded me to the front of the queue at border crossings, adding the full weight of a long line of people to the pressure put on border officials to expedite my travel visas and to not take advantage of the situation (many passengers had murmured to me that, unfortunately, this was often the case). I was only out one more dollar than I had budgeted for visa fees, and moreover, I felt safe and peaceful in the company of the Intercape bus travelers.

As I waited for my kind fellow passengers to pass through immigration, I watched the sun melt into the horizon, launching a crepuscular sky that caught fire like a Flame Lily, as if a handful of cichlids had been tossed out of Lake Malawi and flipped themselves in the air. Soon that great dome overhead turned ruddy and blush, reminding me of sweet potatoes and mangoes and the tangy, pulpy flesh of the granadillas that we bought in the open air markets and bit into after we rubbed their dust onto our jeans. The fading, yet resilient light continued its display, staining the firmament into a mottled lilac—a great, graced ghost of Blantyre's celebrated Jacaranda bloom; then, bluer than the ocean beyond the shores of Robben Island on a clear, chilly June day; and finally, blacker than the small, polished ebony bird that I bought as a keychain on the streets of Bulawayo from the hand of its carver. The sky had been flinging out in all directions its very best show and it was thrilling, but there was nothing like the breathless moments, in the relative quietude of the remote, rural border crossing, when the velvet black sky deepened and tiny pinpoints of light appeared—as quickening as spying the lightning yellow eye of a bat hawk! Soon, before you realized what changes had been happening all around you, the ether had transformed into a rich, inky canvas with crushed diamonds scattered thickly across it and sparkling in the warming breeze. I searched knowingly in vain for the Big Dipper and Cassiopeia. *Okay, can I identify the Southern Cross?* As I beheld the myriad of potential constellations hanging over me, I knew that my ignorance was too great to recognize which stars composed even that basic asterism, so I gently let go of my search and allowed myself to simply enjoy the sheer wonder of a night sky that was new to me. And then the moon rose, with its great, shining, cold, chalky blue light. As I watched the carpet of stars fade in its glow, it struck me that suddenly the sky looked a little more familiar—the patterns of the stars in Africa may not be the same as in America or China or Canada or England or Malta, but the moon was the moon.

One of my seatmates, Beatrice, emerged from the immigration hut, relieved to be through the tedious process. "Come," she called out, waving and beckoning me to rise from my concrete block. "Let's find some food!"

That was an invitation I heartily welcomed. "Yeah!" I sprang up. "But where?"

She pointed to a couple open fires a short walk away. Besides our bus, now waiting for all passengers to pass through to the Zimbabwe side, the working firepits and a nearby shack were the only things that could be seen in the moonlight. "There. That's where food is for sale. There's a toilet in the restaurant, too."

"You mean that little—building?"

"Yes. It's safe. I'll go with you. Do you eat meat?"

"When I can. Where I'm going in Mozambique, I've been told to expect a lot of beans and rice and not much else—which will be okay. I ate a lot of beans and rice in seminary."

"Well, we can get you plenty of beans and rice now if you miss it!" Beatrice laughed. "But if you would like to eat meat here, it will probably be chicken or beef. Zimbabweans eat less fish than Malawians."

"That is no problem! I can wait on fish. My mom and grandma will have plenty of fish ready as soon as I get home."

And so she guided me, into the latest unknown—through the dark, but toward a warm fire and food. Standing by for us as well was the vehicle that would take us one step further on our multi-legged journey, from Malawi and Mozambique, now through Zimbabwe, into South Africa, and—ultimately, for me—to home.

WHEN GRANDMA LOOKED AT THE MOON

* * *

"Mom! What are you doing?" May poked her head through the doorframe into her mother's room. It was evening, and Christina was standing up at the window, both hands on the windowsill. "You should be in bed right now."

"Eh? Why are you up?"

"Mary just called. It's early in the morning in Zimbabwe, but she's got cell phone service while she's traveling through that country, so she just called to say hi. Why are you up?"

"Eh . . . " Christina said, turning her head back toward her view out the window. The tangled silhouettes of a ripe peach tree, a thick-leaved camellia tree, and the top of a redwood fence stood out against the horizon's gray clouds, lit by the rising moon.

"Are you looking at the moon again?"

"Yeah. It's so big."

"I need you to stop standing. You could fall. Can you watch the moon in bed?"

"Not the same."

"Mahh-am!"

"I can't sleep."

"I can tell. You've made your bed very nicely and even put the pillows in place. But I need you to at least sit down."

"I need to keep standing and walking."

May's face softened, and she found herself blinking quickly yet again. Taking a few steps into Christina's bedroom, May picked up a stack of paper resting on one end of a long dresser and approached her mother. "Here, I'll read you some of Mary's emails again. Hold onto my arm and just . . . steady down here . . . " and May eased her mother into a sitting position on the bed.

"I'll lie down," Christina volunteered, and started swinging herself toward a pillow at the head of the bed.

"Okay, let me help you," said May, as she guided her mother's head and then gently lifted her legs.

Christina sighed and rested her eyes. May turned on a small bedside lamp. "Let's see . . . 'Days 27–32. The Motsis returned on Day 28, and I spent the rest of my time in Zim with them. In the daytime, I sat in on some TCZ classes that were distinctively African, whether in teaching style or subject matter. In the afternoons, various people—'"

Cough!

"'. . . various people kindly took me around to parts of Bulawayo—'"

Cough cough!

May paused. "Mom, are you okay?"

Cough! . . . Cough cough cough . . .

In one move, May put the papers on the bed and was on her feet. "I'll get you some albuterol." She swiftly fetched the albuterol and nebulizer from the dresser top, plugged in the nebulizer, and placed the mask over her mother's nose and mouth. The nebulizer trembled as its motor whirred loudly.

Cough.

"Just relax!" May tried to sound calm though she had to shout to be heard above the nebulizer's noise.

. . . Cough . . . Soon Christina's coughs subsided.

"You'll need to take all the medicine, so it will be a few more minutes!"

Christina nodded docilely. After about ten minutes, the nebulizer cup was empty, so May switched it off and turned on the oxygen generator, which was an aural relief as it only hummed. Gingerly but expertly handling the nasal cannula, May inserted its ends into her mother's nostrils.

"Do you want me to keep reading?"

Christina nodded.

May scooped up the stack of email and adjusted her eyeglasses. "So, we are reading about Days 27–32, the second half of Mary's visit to Zimbabwe. Now where did I leave off? Ah, we were just getting started . . . 'In the afternoons, various people kindly took me around to parts of Bulawayo, whether it was to the Motsi daughter's hockey try-outs at the city hockey field, the Western suburbs (where the townships are), or Nesbitt Castle (a one-hundred-ish-yr-old castle built by a former mayor of Bulawayo). And in the evenings, I settled down for very delicious African food in the Motsi home and had good, long talks with Angela and Ray . . . '"

May had become aware of another rhythmic sound joining the hum of the oxygen generator, and she took notice of her mom. Christina was sleeping peacefully—and snoring. The corners of May's mouth turned up gently, and she put down the papers yet again, removed the nasal cannula from her mother's nose, tucked the spare blanket over her (Christina had fallen asleep on top of the usual bedcovers), and clicked off the oxygen generator and bedside lamp. She left the window curtains open, however—in case her mother awoke again and wanted to look at the moon.

7

Sacramento II

I steered the pink wheelchair out of the sun and took a sharp right turn.

"Hold on, Grandma!"

Grandma gripped the armrests of her wheelchair as I pushed her up an incline, her broad-brimmed hat falling back. I had been back home from Africa about two weeks thus far and, rather proudly, had quickly adapted to maneuvering a wheelchair everywhere.

"Ehh, where we going?" Grandma asked, just as there was a roar in the distance.

I paused my feet and swung her hat to the front of her, so that it hung comfortably on her neck by the wind cord. "Hear that, Grandma? I think the lions have finally come out for lunch!"

"Yes. . . . My, my! Are they like the lions that you saw in Africa?"

"Like in Zimbabwe? Eh, I'm pretty sure these lions are bigger, but they are probably fed more. They are also not necessarily recovering from traumatic stuff, like the lions at the rescue were, so they're healthier here." I nodded in the direction of the roaring. "We'll try again to see them on our way out."

"Okay. . . . Where are we going now?"

"Somewhere out of the sun and to some quiet. There are so many people at the zoo today."

Grandma lifted her nose. "I smell something good."

I dropped my gaze and scanned the ground for a few seconds. "Ah, yes! We've entered the Sensory Garden!" I announced, peering closer to a cluster of low-lying identification labels. "There's lavender . . . sage . . . Oh cool, they've put braille on these signs, too, of course. Now I bet there's—yes, here's mint! . . . rosemary . . . fennel . . . You liked cooking with fennel, didn't you, Grandma?"

"Yes. I taught your Mommy, too. It's a good Chinese herb."

"Yes, it's a good herb in many cultures." I had resumed pushing Grandma's wheelchair, and we were now moving alongside a small pond that had been hidden from the main thoroughfare. "Grandma! I can see koi in the pond!"

"I hear water."

"It's the brook running into the koi pond."

"What an interesting place to have at the zoo."

"They designed it especially for zoo visitors who are blind or have difficulty seeing. This is a special place where they can rest, smell, and hear an experience of the zoo." We arrived at a spot with a small bench and a wall of sturdy, towering bamboo that stretched toward the perfect sky. I turned Grandma's wheelchair toward the bench, so I could sit opposite her and also so she could feel sunshine on her face. "You've got the sun on your face. Is that okay?" I checked.

Her eyes were closed. "Feels good!"

I smiled. "Good."

Slightly nervously, I sat down on the bench as Grandma blissfully sunned her face. During the two weeks since I had returned home from backpacking Africa, I had caught up on a small stack of hospice, preparing-for-a-loved-one's-death literature that nurse Stephanie and my mom had collected for our family. I figured it was time to take the advice of those books and take Grandma somewhere peaceful, where we could have a gentle and spiritually mature conversation about how she felt concerning her "transition" and the changes ahead.

"So. Grandma."

"Ehh?" Grandma opened her eyes.

"There's a lot going on these days, isn't there?"

"Sure is! My, my. Yesterday we got ice cream. . . . Today we're at the zoo—"

"—Well, I mean, there's a lot going on in your life these days."

"Ehh? Oh yes! It is busy, busy, busy."

SACRAMENTO II

Hmm. Take two.

"So, Grandma..."

"Ehh?"

"Do you have any... thoughts... about... you know, as you think about eternity... about 'moving on'... about 'being more fully with Jesus'—"

"—*No!!* Don't talk like this!!"

Oops?

"Don't talk like this! Don't think like this!!"

I listened.

"When it's time, I will go. I am not afraid. But don't think like this until He says it is time!"

I nodded. I hadn't expected such a retort from Grandma, but as I sat there for a moment and reflected on her response, she was being totally consistent with her approach to all the major movements of her life. Her faith and commitment to the LORD had always been fearless, deep, and solid, with a childlike simplicity.

" 'kay, well... guess that settles that!"

"Are we going to get something for your brother? From the Kangaroo Café?"

"Sure. Yes. We'll get those garlic fries that he always loves."

"Good."

"It's nice of you to think of that, Grandma." I pushed the wheelchair toward the Sensory Garden exit as another round of roaring erupted from the big cat exhibit. "But first, let's go catch some lions!"

***

Dear Rayeesha,

Hey, dear friend! I'm sorry it's taken me so long to write back. I pretty much hit the ground running with hospice care for my grandma when I got home from Africa.

Firstly, huge congrats on your and Gregory's engagement!! (Hey Gregory, if you are reading this over Rayeesha's shoulder, I'm proud of you and you know the truth of it—you are a super lucky and blessed man!! Seriously, I love you both and am so happy for you guys!!) Send me your wedding date when you have it; I'm admittedly really swamped right now, but if I plan ahead, I should be able to be there. Know that I want to be there!

Secondly, thank you again for praying for me while I was backpacking around Africa! As you know, we all at the Clicks store in Gaborone especially benefitted from your and Gregory's prayers. The second day there was not quite as crazy as the first, but after that instance when the customer fainted in the store while I was away at lunch, I realized that the people were too dependent on me. Though I had told them all along that they did not need me and could be doing this themselves, they still did not try to really help or pray for the customer until I returned. No matter what I told them and even though I stayed away from the store for long breaks that day, they did not believe that they did not need me. It was a long and still somewhat unresolved grief for me, that the Clicks community saw too much of me and not enough of the LORD, who was really the one who healed them.

There were a lot more twists and turns in the journey than I had expected—not only in Africa but also at home—and I think I got back to Sacramento just in time. The adjustment from backpacking adventures to full-time hospice caring appears pretty dramatic on the outside, I know, but to me, the differences are superficial and the transition has felt very natural. While I was away, my mom and I managed to stay in touch most days, and she kept me posted on how my grandma was doing. Even deeper than that, there's honestly a sort of desperation in both what I was doing two-plus months ago and what I'm doing now—they're sink or swim situations when it comes to prayer and dependence on the LORD! So, the most vital dynamic—that between God and oneself—has pretty much remained the same, and thanks be to God that it has. There is no sweeter, no greater relationship or way to be!

Meanwhile, in the past two-ish months, I've become adept at changing my grandma's diapers and pads, brushing her (few) teeth, taking apart and putting back together again her wheelchair, dumping and cleaning her portable potty, putting in her oxygen tube, etc. My brother and I are now alternating being on "night duty"—that is, sleeping on a mattress on the floor of Grandma's room to keep her company and help her if she needs it during the night (her modesty so far has prevented her from waking up my brother when she uses the loo at night, but when I'm on duty it can be as often as four to six times a night). I've also started taking informal Portuguese lessons (I was introduced to the language at the orphanage in Mozambique) and am developing a course on the book of Proverbs that I'll teach next year in Canada. I know it's a lot—caring for someone in hospice and trying to keep up with my usual interests and vocation. God knows, I may well need to drop or put on pause some, if not all, of these projects if my grandmother's needs become greater. That's okay—I know my priorities. Ultimately, if it comes down to it, someone else can volunteer at the orphanage in Mozambique, and someone else can teach at the college in Canada. Few people but family and close friends (and, of course, medical and caregiving professionals, like Grandma's hospice nurse, Stephanie) can be here for my grandma in this critical and highly vulnerable stage of life, and one is not always blessed with this opportunity to come alongside and support a loved one so beneficially in this way. Don't get me wrong—this is super hard. None of the three of us could adequately care for my grandma on our own, not by a long shot! But it is also very much a privilege.

In the interests of my grandma—who is the most extroverted of us all—we've become members of the local zoo, and as the late summer days have turned into golden autumn ones near our corner of the valley, we've become regulars at the fishing pond at Apple Hill. It's a bit of a drive, because the apple farms are slightly up into the mountains, but it is also a lovely one and affords us a very nice day trip together if we plan it well (i.e., bring diaper pads and oxygen tank). My grandma has always loved fishing, especially with my granddad when he was alive. She used to do the whole works—catch, clean, and cook the thing—but she hasn't done much of any of that lately for obvious reasons. So, Grandma, Mom, Ben, and I take a team approach to fishing now: Grandma holds the line and waits for the fish; when she gets a good tug, Ben or Mom helps her reel the thing in; the fishing booth at the apple farms cleans out the fish; we make sure Grandma gets handed her cleaned fish in a bag, which she proudly hands to my mom; Mom cooks the fish when we get home; and we all eat the fish and rightly compliment Grandma on her fishing skills while reflecting on the splendid day that we've spent together in the fresh air, forests, and apple orchards of the foothills. That has become our bi-weekly routine, and it's been good for our hearts, particularly my grandma's. As my mom says, if we don't get Grandma outside, she'll die inside.

I've got to get my grandma out on her late afternoon walk now, but keep me posted on your wedding prep! Really glad to hear that Gregory is thriving in law school, especially now that the regular academic year is underway.

Much love to you both!
Mary xo

* * *

"Are we going to see the ducks?" Grandma asked.

I tried not to sound like I was making an effort as I steadied the wheelchair down the hill while answering my grandma. "That is up to you, Grandma! Which way do you want to go? If we go to the right, we'll go to the canals and see the ducks. If we go to the left, we'll go through more of the greenbelt and over a couple bridges. The sun is pretty low in the sky, so we'll have to choose—we don't have time for both, unfortunately."

Grandma raised an arm and pointed left toward a long stretch of seemingly endless grass and dense redwood trees with a smooth concrete path meandering through it.

"Okay!" I said, veering the wheelchair left. Grandma had chosen a section of the greenbelt that I loved, for it was the greenest and most forested part of the park. But, for that same reason, it was also the coldest and darkest area of the greenbelt near the end of the day. We would need to move quickly.

I speed-rolled Grandma in her pink wheelchair along the curves of the path, nodding and smiling with gratitude at the presence of a handful of friendly passersby pushing babies in their strollers, walking cute little dogs in sweaters, and snagging last-minute walks like we were; I was glad we were not entirely alone. As we rounded a corner with a lofty and noble redwood spreading its prodigious leaves over part of the walkway, I called out, "Smell that, Grandma?" and took a deep breath that was noisy enough so she could hear what I was doing. I saw Grandma lift her head to inhale the fresh evergreen scent. I did not slow down our pace, however.

"Did you smell it?" I asked.

"Yes. So nice!"

"Hold on! We've got a couple small bumps on the path, and then we're going up our first bridge."

Now an experienced wheelchair rider, Grandma automatically grabbed the armrests as her knitted hat bounced on her head. We had enough inertia that we mounted the first bridge fairly easily. At the top, I swiftly turned the wheelchair 180° and positioned myself to walk the wheelchair backwards down the other side of the bridge—when I glanced up and paused. I was now facing the dense redwood patch we had just woven our way through, and I could see that the patch was only going to get darker—and do so soon—with the fading daylight.

"Sorry, Grandma, we're only going to do one bridge today. We need to get home while there's still light out." And I grasped the wheelchair's handlebars to turn Grandma halfway around again.

"No!" Grandma held out a hand.

What?

"Everything okay?" I asked.

Grandma's hand was still extended. "Stop."

I peered over the bridge. No sign of an automobile accident. In fact, there were barely any cars on the street below.

"Wait," she said.

I surveyed the skyline in the direction of Grandma's outstretched hand. "Is it . . . the sunset?" I asked.

"Yes," she said slowly, her hand lifting and lowering as she said that word, her eyes entranced by the warm robin's-breast orange and ginkgo gold glow filling the western end of the sky. Her breathing had relaxed so much that I kept a watchful eye on her face, shining in the golden hour lambency, and fretted to myself that I should have brought her eyeglasses. Yet, somehow, Grandma seemed to see everything she needed to.

"It's beautiful, isn't it?"

"Yes."

We stayed there on top of the bridge for about three minutes, silent—a wrinkled little grandma in a small, sweetly-colored wheelchair and her adult granddaughter standing protectively behind her with hands holding fast to its handlebars. Scattered birds flew overhead to their homes for rest as we were washed in the great fuchsia-pink luminosity of the waning cinnabar orb on the horizon. We watched, rapt, as it slipped through a light scattering of clouds and nearly out of view.

"Okay," she said softly.

"It's time to go home?" I asked.

Grandma nodded.

"You sure?"

"Yes."

The clouds overhead started to radiate and flush a bright purple-red—like the stains of blueberry juice on our hands after we picked the berries from my mom's bushes—which brightened the sky. I was grateful for the added moments of light, whispered a short prayer as I turned Grandma and her wheelchair around, and headed us back down the bridge. When we got to the bottom, I tucked Grandma's hat over her ears and sped us into the shadows of our beloved redwood canopy. Still silently praying, I said aloud to my grandma, "It'll be a little dark, but we'll get home soon."

"Okay." Grandma did not sound afraid.

* * *

Tablet computer journal:

October 5th, Saturday.

I "woke up" today around 4 p.m. Mom and Ben must have been in here several times already, but their kind sounds did not wake me up. Poor Grandma had a rough night, and even as I write this, she is lying in bed taking in the difficult current reality that there is something wrong with her body. Desperate to help Grandma stop fidgeting and turning in bed, I laid in her hospice bed with her, and we prayed together as she coped with not understanding why she is so restless. She asked why I was lying there with her, and I thought quickly and said that I liked being there with her (which was true enough, though I was really just trying to help her calm down). She said, "I like you here, too. It makes me so I don't feel . . . miserable!"

I asked her what she wanted me to tell her future great grandchildren. "Whatever you like." I listed off some good memories of Grandma.

"How you and Grandpa met . . . and that you rode an elephant in Thailand—"

"I don't know. I think so."

"How you were a missionary to children in Asia—"

"*That* I did!"

"You came to England and one of my graduations."

"I don't remember so well."

"You went to Israel with us. Remember that? We did that together."

"We went to Jerusalem and the Dead Sea."

"Yes, that's right, Grandma!"

"The Dead Sea is not so deep as people think. You can walk in it."

"Yes, that's true, Grandma! You walked in it, remember?"

"Yes."

"You walked in it with Ben! And you even floated in it!"

"Yes."

SACRAMENTO II

* * *

Surrounded by "Happy Birthday!" mylar balloons, flowers, medications, bandages, and hygiene supplies, Stephanie the hospice nurse sat on the edge of Grandma's bed, picked up her very aged feet, and massaged them. She was somehow nonplussed by the fact that she was wearing a pretty, flowery dress while handling my grandma's feet on her lap.

"This is a great way to bring comfort to someone," Steph said to me and Ben, but beaming at Grandma as her thumb rubbed into the knots of her feet. "How is that, Mrs. Fong?"

"Ohhh, sooo good," Grandma responded, blissfully flat on her back with her hands folded on her stomach and her eyes closed.

"Have you ever tried massaging your grandma's feet?"

"Uh, no," replied Ben.

"Me, neither," I confessed.

"We cut her toenails, clean her feet, and bandage sores on her feet when she has them," Ben noted, in our defense, "but we haven't massaged them."

"Yeah, what he said," I awkwardly supported.

"Ohhhh . . . " Grandma repeated.

Ben and I shared guilty looks.

"Well," said Steph in a relaxed and uncondemning voice, "you should try it sometime." She stroked down the wrinkled lines of Grandma's feet a few more times, eyes rapt and delighted with the effect of her work on Grandma. With a gentle circular motion reflective of her yoga exercises, Steph scooped Grandma's feet off her lap and settled them onto the bed. Her eyes twinkled as she attended to her client, as peaceful as the surface of a koi pond on a mild winter day.

"You seem pretty relaxed, Mrs. Fong."

"Yehhsss . . . " came the voice from my barely conscious grandma.

"Would you like to stay here and take a nap?"

"Yehhsss. . . . Thank you."

Steph turned to our family. "Okay," she said quietly, "Let's go to the dining room, where we can talk more."

It was a brilliant move on Stephanie's part. While Grandma snoozed, we debriefed with the hospice nurse about Grandma's two-week E. coli infection, her three falls, constipation, diarrhea, and increasing loss of many basic functional abilities.

"The scariest moment for me," I shared, clutching my hands together and leaning on the little round table, "was a couple days ago when Grandma vomited in her sleep. I was on duty at that time, and I woke up hearing her choking. I jumped up from the mattress on the floor, yelled for my mom to come help, and got over to my grandma. As soon as I got to her, I rolled her to her side, but in those few seconds before I got to her, she was so tired and weak that she just lay there, not moving. Her vomit was soaking into her hair and clothes and bedsheets—she was too tired to be able to do anything about it."

Steph listened and nodded compassionately. "You are an amazing family. You all know that I have wondered these past few months how Mrs. Fong can function outwardly as well as she does when internally her conditions have indicated she should be doing otherwise. She certainly is doing better than anyone has expected! As I've often said: your grandmother is not a textbook case! But there's no question she couldn't have done it all without you guys. She's a true 'old soul'; she's holding on because of you all, her family." Steph paused, then resumed with a sly wink, "You know, she's technically bed-ridden—except you guys keep taking her out!"

"Meh, let's see," Ben began. "Last week Mary took Grandma early Christmas shopping at the mall . . . "

"Mom and I took her to the Crocker Art Gallery with church friends the day after that," I continued. "Then Ben took Grandma for a drive along the Sacramento River toward the Delta to see the fall colors."

"We all went fishing," Mom piped in. "And together we caught three fish!"

"This week is busier," I noted. "Since this is Grandma and Mom's birthday week!"

"It is," Steph affirmed, smiling behind the orchid plant that she had brought for Grandma's birthday. "She's . . . " Steph leaned forward and scanned her laptop screen. "Ninety-five years old!"

"Yeah, we think so. She was born in the old country, so she didn't have a birth certificate," Ben clarified, "but her parents kept track of the date. Grandma was pretty certain about November 5. We think we're within a year, if not exactly on it."

"Well, your grandma has certainly lived a good, full life—thanks in no small part to you, her family!"

"I—I hope we don't miss it when her life among us closes," I said quietly. "I think her greatest fear is dying alone. . . . I don't want her to suffer through pain or agony alone, neglected and just wilting away."

"I doubt that will happen with your grandma," Steph casually remarked, sifting through her bag for a small box of medication. "Most people die in the same way in which they lived."

I blinked. *Hey, that was deep!*

Steph chattered away in an upbeat tone, seemingly unaware that she had just dropped a profundity bomb on us. " 'kay, I really doubt you're going to need this soon, but just in case, here are a few Scop patches. Use these on your grandma if it looks like she's going fast."

"How will we know?" I asked.

"The death rattle."

"What's it sound like?" Ben probed further.

"Exactly that—a rattle. The sound is unlike anything else; you'll know it when you hear it."

"Great," I responded, as Mom took the little box of Scop patches. Steph gave me a sympathetic pat on the shoulder.

"Are you still planning to go to your conference in a couple weeks?" Stephanie asked me as she packed her laptop.

"The Society of Biblical Literature conference? Yes, though I'll only go to half the conference—enough to stay in touch with colleagues and what's going on in the academy."

"Good. I'm glad you're doing that."

I paused, then included: "I'm taking a break from Portuguese lessons so I can be home in the evenings more. I'm okay with that."

Steph nodded. "You'll know." She turned to my mom and brother. "Any special plans for your grandma's birthday week?"

"Tomorrow the home health carer will give my mom her sponge bath, and then the wound care nurse will evaluate her sores," Mom answered.

"Then we'll go to the cemetery to put flowers on Dad's grave," Ben added. "And after that, we'll visit the local fish hatchery. Grandma will like that."

* * *

A few days later, as the sun rose, I spied my brother at the end of the dark hallway. Since he and I had assumed night duties for Grandma, we were not responsible for her morning care, let alone feeding her breakfast (by this point, Grandma's breakfast was organic baby food or pureed fare). No, breakfast was Mom's special connection time with Grandma. But on this occasion, a few days after Grandma's birthday, with the half-deflated helium balloons floating around her hospice bed at mid-height, my sleep-deprived brother was not concerned about whose duty or shift it was. Ben just wanted his grandmother loved and fed. As he spoon-fed her, fresh sunlight spilled onto her bed and illuminated her. No words passed between them, but I could see Grandma lift her arms and draw circles in the air in between munching on spoonfuls from Ben. She had not given up her old habit of moving her arms to maintain strength and circulation, though we had grown accustomed to her face being unusually still from muscle atrophy. Yet despite that, I could tell by the angle of her head that her eyes were fixed on the caring and concerned face of my brother, who gently and patiently waited for her to chew and swallow before he bent down and fed her another teaspoonful.

The light on Grandma that morning was so bright and bountiful that her hair and the blanket tucked around her shone white, and whenever my brother leaned over to feed her, the light reflected and radiated white on his eyeglasses, the tiny glass jar of baby food he was holding, and the comfortable pajamas he was still wearing. Grandma's effulgence did not stop there; it threw blinding light onto everything that surrounded them—the wall, the floor, the open door with my unstained diamond willow staff leaning behind it, even the portable potty. I held my breath and, mesmerized, gazed down the hall some moments longer, not wanting to disturb something so remarkable, so tender, so delicate, so vulnerable, so powerful.

A shiny red balloon floated into my line of view, blocking my vision of Grandma and Ben. It was okay. The moment was theirs, and I had been granted a glimpse of a private conversation. I tiptoed away to the kitchen.

8

Christmas Day, 2013

CHRISTMAS DAY, 2013

Dear friends,

Grandma died about four hours ago. Ish. When she stopped breathing, she still had a pulse for awhile. Mom left the room to call Auntie Lillian and her friends in the Moms Prayer Group, and Ben asked for a few minutes alone with Grandma's body. Ben had also asked if I wanted a few minutes alone with Grandma's body, and I had said no, but when Ben left the room, I went in and stayed there for another three and a half hours. Since I could still sense life in her body, I wasn't sure if her spirit had entirely departed. So, I played the second movement of the Bruch Violin Concerto on my violin (Granddad's favorite) and "Higher Throne" on my guitar (when I wasn't choking on tears) and read aloud passages from her old Bible—First Corinthians 5 and the book of Revelation. As I got up to finally eat, my brother had awoken from his nap and appeared in the doorway. He was trying to decide whether to finish composing his now belated Christmas cards in Grandma's room or in the family room where he had been writing earlier last week. So, now I am sitting in a cozy little space on the floor on one side of Grandma's bed with Grandma's Bible, Ben's handwritten Christmas card to her, my guitar, my laptop, potstickers for dinner, and a box of tissues. Ben is on the other side of the bed, sitting on Grandma's adjustable shower chair (which is obviously no longer in the shower; that ended months ago, when she was switched to sponge baths) and tapping away at the keys on his laptop, which itself is perched on the TV tray that has doubled for the past several months as a stand for hospice materials and as his temporary desk in this room. His laptop is playing a tranquil mix of the ukulele music that Grandma loved so much in her last months with us. And every once in awhile one of us will ask or say a thought—Where do you think Grandma's spirit is right now? Going to the zoo again is going to be hard. Should we tell our pastor before hospice takes her body away? Has it sunk in for you yet? How's Mom doing?, etc. Then we process a bit together. And, of course, we are wearing our new sweaters . . .

Up to a couple days ago, Grandma had found living as we know it to be physically tough, but she still seemed to want to live. Her vitals had continued to be reasonably strong (relative to her conditions), and we all thought she was going to make it at least through the holidays. But yesterday, Grandma slept through nearly the whole day and her excess secretion level was significantly and audibly worse. When Ben woke her up so that I could feed her, he could tell that she was not doing well, and he basically sounded the alarm that she had the "death rattle." Oh man, this death rattle thing. On and off for the past several months hospice had thought Grandma had it, but then the sound would abate after a day or two. So, we've been plenty aware of what the death rattle is, and it's just as they say—when you hear it, you know what it is; you can't mistake it. With Grandma's eyes closed most of the time, we couldn't tell the difference between when she was asleep snoring and when she was awake—the sound was the same. This time, it persisted long enough that I rang the emergency nurse. He said it was time to use the Scop patch and gave me a plan for Grandma's new course of treatment for the next week. That was yesterday, Christmas Eve.

Thanks to the earlier advice of Grandma's hospice nurse, I was prepared to administer the patch, even as I knew that it was a this-is-pretty-much-the-end treatment. I gently adhered the patch behind Grandma's ear and, though I could not tell if she could hear me, I prayed for her as I always did when it was time to sleep for the first half of the night. I told her that we would miss her, but it was okay if it was time for her to be more fully with Jesus. Clicking off the bedside lamp, I kissed Grandma's forehead and quietly slipped out to eat a very late bite of dinner and go to an 11 p.m. candlelight Christmas Eve service at church. When I returned home, Ben and I turned Grandma onto her side, changed her diaper, covered her bedsores, tended to her feet (which were actually healing from sores), tried to brush her teeth, etc. Having thus spent the first five-plus hours of Christmas Day quite awake and active, I was ready to crash. Ben put his Christmas card for Grandma next to her bed so she could see it. I added a gold-wrapped Christmas present next to it and went to sleep.

Seven hours later, I woke up and went to Grandma's room. Grandma was still asleep, and Ben was still asleep, lying partly on the floor and partly on the futon mattress at the foot of Grandma's bed, a vision of physical and emotional exhaustion in the morning sunlight. Meanwhile, even though she had the patch on and had had several rounds of a supplemental medication throughout the night, Grandma sounded worse than before. But, unlike the day before, she opened her eyes and pretty much kept them open, even when she apparently couldn't focus. We sat Grandma upright and tried to feed her and give her water. We moistened her mouth and tried to clean some of the phlegm out of it. I gave her morphine for the pain. Mom came in and was concerned about the phlegm, so we turned Grandma to her other side. I sat in this nook that I am sitting in now so that Grandma could see me while she was on her side, and I played Doerksen's "Eternity" for the thirtieth time on my laptop and guitar. I paused to get some breakfast from the kitchen, and Ben resumed writing his Christmas card letters on the other side of Grandma's bed.

I did a few small trips between the living room and Grandma's bedroom to bring a collection of Christmas presents that would be relevant to her—cheerfully wrapped gifts for Grandma or from Grandma or from people Grandma has known for a long time were scattered on her bed. I fetched my mom, and in a rare circumstance (apart from meetings with a hospice worker), all three of us happened to be gathered together around Grandma's bed. It was a festive and fun time! We took turns opening presents, including presents for Grandma. The first present we opened was the gold-wrapped box that I had placed in front of her the night before. Inside was a pearl necklace.

"Put it in her hand," said my mom, excitedly. "Grandma loves pearls." I nodded and wrapped the necklace gently around Grandma's hand.

We shifted quickly through the rainbow splash of packages on her bed, holding up things with masses of springy curled ribbons and jangling little bells. Here's a present for Mom from . . . ! Here's a present for Ben from . . . ! Oh, hey Grandma! "Here's a present for you from your son Peter and your daughter-in-law Sarah! See, they thought of you on Christmas and wanted to give you something." And so on.

"Here's a present for Mom, from . . . Grandma!" I cried out, extending a thin, green-and-white package with a mop of ribbon on top.

"From Grandma??" asked Mom, nearly laughing with incredulity as she took the slender gift.

"Yes, when I took Grandma early Christmas shopping in late October, she told me that you need money, so she wanted me to give you a gift card for groceries."

"Oh! Thank you, Mom!" And Mom kissed Grandma on the forehead. "I love you!"

Grandma's response was to slightly turn her head toward her daughter and—with determination—keep her eyes open, even though her body now heaved with the difficulty she had breathing.

At the same time, I was aware that our magnum opus was coming up: Amidst all the happy ripping of colorful Christmas wrap and shiny ribbon and thank-you's and look-who-this-is-from exclamations, I had been carefully withholding the present that Grandma would most care about, waiting until near the end of all the gifts opening in hope of maintaining her attention through this special family time. I was already quite surprised that, after nearly an entire Christmas Eve with her eyes closed, Grandma had managed to keep them open now for the past three-ish hours. But now it was time, for I did not want to risk stretching Grandma's energy level by delaying further. For weeks I had been reminding Grandma during our wheelchair-pushing walks, as we ambled by inflatable snowmen and twinkle-light-covered reindeer on neighbors' lawns, that she had already taken care of getting Christmas presents for people. I assured my habitually giving grandmother that she was ahead of the gift-giving game and had absolutely nothing to worry about. She had never said anything in response, and I honestly figured that what I was saying was rather lost in her age-related dementia and the happy distractions of tinsel-and-bauble-wrapped Christmas trees that bedizened every window we walked by. Still, I suspected that, if anything, Grandma's care was most invested in the box that I handed to my brother.

"To Ben, from . . . Grandma!"

"Oh! From Grandma?" Ben gave me a quizzical look.

"Yes! From Grandma!" I said, holding out the large, long-ish, red box with holly sprigs printed on it.

"Oh! Thank you, Grandma!" Ben said loudly, to assure that Grandma could hear his gratitude.

Ben lifted up the box and beheld it from one end to the other. "Wow, it's so nicely wrapped!" He set it on his lap and carefully shimmied off the ribbons. "These are nice ribbons!" He started to slowly tear the scotch tape, articulating aloud as he did so, "I'm trying to save the wrapping paper—"

I grew impatient. "—Uh, you wanna open it up?"

"Okay, okay!" my brother said with a laugh. But he was loving and wise to take his time and to appreciate vocally every aspect of unwrapping that gift. Even if Grandma couldn't see through her glazed-over eyes, she could hear. "Okay, I'm uncovering the box!"

We waited.

Wide folds of wrapping paper crinkled and warped as they were tossed to the ground. And then: "Grandma got me something from GAP??"

"Yeah, we went early Christmas shopping together."

"Were these expensive?" He was staring at two new, fine GAP sweaters lying neatly in the opened box on his lap.

I had to tell the truth. "Yeah. She wouldn't let me get you anything on sale. She insisted on exactly what's in that box, and wouldn't let them go!"

"Can Grandma afford them?"

Pause. "We, uh, made it work."

Unsurprisingly by now, Ben spent much time kindly appreciating every little aspect of those sweaters—from carefully cutting off the tags to reading the washing instructions so as to figure out exactly what the sweaters' colors are called. In the meantime, I went ahead with opening another couple presents, including the sweater that Grandma had gotten for me. Then it was my turn to get to thank Grandma and remind her of what a great provider she had been to me. So much was going on—Ben was now standing in front of Grandma's very large mirror and dresser, trying on the second sweater; I had just tossed on my sweater from Grandma and was appraising it in the closet door mirror; Mom was sitting next to Grandma's bed the whole time just being with her and admiring everything; all sorts of Christmas wrap, ribbon, bells, dried fruit, and chocolate were strewn across the futon mattress below.

And then, amid the sounds of Grandma's strained, secretion-full breathing and our peals of excited appreciation, it was suddenly quiet. Ben, somehow acutely aware that Grandma had gone silent, immediately stopped and in a hushed, urgent voice said, "Mary." I whirled around and stared at Grandma. Less than half a minute ago, I had been semi-aware that Grandma had just let out three little cough-breaths—compared to two days ago, it seemed like such a small thing. But then that was it. Her breathing did not resume as usual. Her chest was still. The labored heaving was over. Mom and I checked her pulse. It was still there, and incredibly fast. And then weak. And then barely perceptible. Ben and I automatically sat on her bed and took her hands.

We sang "Jesus Loves Me" and "Angels We Have Heard on High." With all good intentions, Mom hurried out to bring us monetary Christmas presents from Grandma, but it seemed too late. I didn't know how to respond and looked at my brother, who had a tear falling.

"That can wait for later," he almost whispered.

"Yeah," I agreed. I was too choked up to say more.

"I'm going to need some time first."

"Yeah."

And you know the rest.

She died with pearls in her hand. (Well, yes, and also with her grandchildren's hands in her hands. <3) Even as I type this, the pearls are still in her hand.

After a lifetime of poverty, dysfunctional family, discrimination, and then chosen humility to serve the poor in her senior years, she ended her life surrounded by love, joy, hope, and faith. In the last seasons of her life, she fulfilled lifelong dreams and wishes that brought out the child in her that had never been safe enough to come out until then. We were blessed not only to provide her an emotionally safe home, but a loving one that could also provide for all the physical needs that she had had to be concerned about for ninety-plus years. And we got to give her experiences, memories, and—most of all—love that she never had to doubt was there for her.

I was so blessed to see—and to *know*—that Grandma, in so many ways, died with pearls in her hand (cf. Matt. 13:44–46; Rev. 21:21).

I think it's super cool that my Grandma died on Christmas Day. Mom was born on Grandma's birthday; Granddad died the day after Grandma's birthday (the doctors had expected him to die on her birthday, but she prayed it wouldn't happen on that day); and my Dad died on Grandma's birthday. So, a lot has revolved around Grandma's birthday. But Grandma revolved around the LORD. As Auntie Lillian emailed tonight:

CHRISTMAS DAY, 2013

> I believe Mom [i.e., Grandma] was waiting for Christmas. Jesus was born this day and now Mom has gone to Heaven this day to be with him. God bless us all. She's at peace.

Indeed, Christmas Day reminds us that God came into the world so that we can be with Him forever. Grandma, in life and in death, took up this offer and came to Him. As always, she has been and ever will be with the LORD. As Grandma put it some months before she died, "God rules on earth. God rules in Heaven. It is all the same."

True Christmas blessings to you and yours now and forevermore.

9

The Zoo

It was Day 8.

On Day 3, Mom and I took a walk in the greenbelt, and I took her to the bridge where Grandma and I had watched the sunset. The three of us went to church together on Day 5. Ben and I fed the ducks at the canals on Day 6. All had gone much more calmly than I had expected, and there weren't many special Grandma-shared places left to meaningfully revisit. Except the zoo. I figured it was time, and I braced myself internally. This one I would do alone.

It was a sunny, but cold day, so I bundled up in my mittens and Grandma's knit hat, then proceeded directly to William Land Park. I parked our car at my favorite area for unloading and setting up Grandma's wheelchair. Normally, dealing with her wheelchair took several minutes, so it seemed far too fast and easy to just walk from the car to the zoo entrance. Instead, I stood there behind the car for awhile, just remembering the mechanics of assembling the little pink wheelchair. I traced our old route from the park to the zoo, and continued to follow that path—invisible, but so clearly delineated in my mind—as it entered the zoo and wove through exhibits and animal dens. I paused at the tigers, the giraffes, the gorillas, the red pandas, the outdoor tropical fish tank. I took hushed footsteps into the Sensory Garden, not wanting to make a sound or even breathe as the ground felt holy. I sat down on the bench in the shade of a Japanese maple and with the wall of green bamboo behind me. *Yeah. Okay. This isn't bad. I'm surprised I'm not really feeling anything.* So, after a short while, I got up and left.

THE ZOO

There was only one thing remaining on the route that Grandma and I would take through the zoo, and that was the Kangaroo Café. Grandma and I had a tradition of getting garlic fries from there to bring home for Ben.

I was there before the lunch rush, so there was no wait in line. I put in my order, faintly smiled and awkwardly muttered to the polite cashier that "they were a tradition of my Grandma," stood to the side in front of an empty cash register while I waited for the fries, and felt a few tears well up in my face (but not enough to cry if I wanted). I got the fries double-wrapped in cellophane for the drive home, and walked uneventfully through and out of the zoo. I unlocked the car and proceeded to get in—rather too easily, as there was no Grandma to gently ease into the passenger seat and buckle up, and no wheelchair to haul to its side, disassemble, and carefully pack into the trunk. So, I stepped out and paused respectfully again outside the car, then re-entered it and headed home.

Somewhere along the bend of the wide concrete highway that is I-5, I surprised myself by getting misty-eyed. *What odd timing*, I thought. *Can't be much, though. I'm almost home. This little mission is almost over.* I turned two corners to reach our street and was fighting back tears. I pushed the button on the garage door opener and pulled into our driveway, barely able to see. I finally wiped away some of the water in my eyes, just so I could safely get the car into the garage.

Mom was standing at the door, waiting to welcome me home. I walked up to her with Grandma's hat pulled over my ears and holding out the wrapped garlic fries on a mittened hand as I choked on tears. "Got—some—*choke*—garlic fries—*choke*—for Ben." And, still extending the package of garlic fries to her, I sobbed.

"Oh! I know, I know . . . " Mom cried, as she rushed past the screen door and gave me a big hug. "I miss her, too."

We stood there awhile, no more words needed, weeping and in a big bear hug of Mom, me, and the garlic fries that Grandma never forgot for Ben.

10

The Outskirts of Musanze

"What an experience to see the gorillas—two silverbacks, the teenage twins, and the baby! I know this is off-peak season, but it's still totally worth it," I enthused as I flopped on the backseat of the jeep. The patchy, dark emerald fabric of the cool, dense forest we were driving alongside rolled by as whisps of colorful *kitenges* punctuated the scene. I sat up and peered through the windshield, waving at passersby, who smiled and waved back. I was a long way from home, but the gracious hospitality of so many of the people whom I met in Africa always made me feel welcome and understood in a way that I didn't experience elsewhere.

So here I was in Rwanda. It had been a month and one week since Grandma had passed away, and despite the special place of Africa in my heart, the last place any of us had imagined I would be soon after her passing would be Rwanda. But I was sparked by my previous Africa backpacking trip, a fragile scrawl I had discovered in the back of Grandma's Bible, and an unusually heavy burden on my heart that God had some reason He wanted me to go to Rwanda soon. Thus, I decided to squeeze in a short, relaxed, and fairly mellow trip there before I would resume teaching. In this way, I hoped to fulfill the last of Grandma's final wishes, as set forth in that handwritten will of hers in her Bible back cover: to give her clothing to overseas missions. I found an indigenous Christian Rwandan NGO that I could visit and that would gladly receive Grandma's clothing for AIDS- and genocide widows, in addition to a suitcase full of Christian seminary books and commentaries from my pastor. While I would be in the country, a guided hike into the wild-celery-covered forests of the Virunga Mountains to see the endangered mountain gorillas sounded good and salubrious for the soul (plus, I had heard that the gorilla permit prices might double in the near future, so I figured the timing was particularly felicitous). That was all. It seemed to be a reasonably restful, simple plan.

"I'm just so hungry now," I remarked. "I can't wait to get back to the dining room at the lodge!"

"Ah, but we must visit the cultural village first, remember?" my very able driver of now four days, Theodore, reminded me. "Don't you want to see a traditional king's palace? And how to shoot a bow and arrow? And the medicine man? They are all families of former poachers working in this cultural village. You must go!"

"Oh my gosh, Theodore, but I've hardly eaten since six this morning and just did two days of bush-whacking through three climate zones—on Mt. Karasimbi! I only had half a granola bar for lunch 'cause I gave the other half to my porter. I've gotta sleep."

"This is a distinctive of our tours! The cultural village will only be ten minutes away from the lodge. We can keep it short, but you must go!"

I clammed up for a moment, suddenly realizing that it would be rude of me not to go. But I genuinely did not know if I could walk or even stay awake much longer.

"You promise it will be short? Like, no more than a half hour. You promise!"

"No more than a half hour. Promise. Remember: You have a goat to give to a needy family."

Oh man, what a cincher. Theodore was right—the goat gifting was important. In order to give the goat to a needy family and be culturally polite, I would muster the energy for a half hour visit. I could do it. I *would* do it. "But remember! No more than a half hour!"

"Yes! I promise! I'll even call them right now and let them know it will only be a half hour." Theodore pulled out his cell phone and kept an eye on the road.

"Oh, and Theodore—ask them if their medicine man is a Christian or not. If he's not a Christian, I don't want to see him."

"The medicine men at this place are all Christian here. No problem."

"A half hour!" I was determined to make the point indelible, even if it would drive us both crazy.

"Yes, a half hour!"

Riding down a very bumpy, dusty road—what Theodore half-jokingly shouted over the jeep's rumbling was referred to as "African massage"— I admitted to myself that perhaps I had had too romantic an expectation for a gentle trip in Africa. At the same time, as I coughed and gripped my stomach in the dust and diesel of the sometimes chaotic journey, I could not deny that I savored breathing in the frosty early morning dew before the sun rose in this "land of a thousand hills," and I never ceased to be entranced by its many-terraced, grassy slopes laced with mist and smokestacks and scattered with dazzling sunbirds that sparkled and trilled when daylight broke through the haze of the western highlands and Lake Kivu beyond. Yes, of course, the mountain gorilla viewing was a humbling privilege, as was exploring the land. But the greatest encounter I had found thus far on this journey was surely to engage with the resilient and deeply-hearted people of central and western Rwanda who shared with me their stories of survival, exile, loss, and the choice to recover as a nation.

We slowed to a stop in a clearing as spare, lithe men ran past us. My eye followed their route into a wide, spacious area ahead surrounded by a low wall of small, rough-cut boulders. Theodore and I got out of the jeep and made our way over an extremely rocky path along the stone wall. How in the world those men had run so nimbly down this difficult path was beyond me, and I was reminded that this was their land, and I was fortunate to visit.

"Do you hear that?" Theodore asked me as he helped steady me on the path.

"What?" I asked, not taking my eyes off the ground as I navigated my way over the jumble of rocks.

"'Baahhh, baahhh.' It's your goat!"

I glanced up, and sure enough, there inside the entrance of the cultural community village was a handsome goat tied with a rope to the welcome sign. A short man immaculately dressed was already standing by the sign and the goat to greet us.

"Good afternoon, and welcome to our cultural community village! I am Emmanuel, and I am the manager here. This village has been here for ten years, and I have been manager here for seven years! Now, I understand that we only have a short time to show you our village, so if I may, I will begin now and introduce you to our village!" With a gracious wave of his hand towards huts and booths in the distance, Emmanuel launched into an overview of the site.

"First, we will go to the King's House, where you can see the rooms inside, hear our traditional stories about kings in the past, and be king for a day through a traditional ceremony! Next, we have musical instruments. See that lineup of drums? You can play one! We will introduce you to our traditional songs. After that, we have some old types of hunting techniques. You can learn how to use a bow and arrow. These, our former gorilla poachers will show you—they no longer poach but use their strength for traditional dancing and to show how our forebears used to hunt."

I had been listening with great interest, interjecting mm-hmms and yeses as Emmanuel gave this impressive list. He continued, "We have a medicine man—"

"—*Okay, wait!*" I started back a little. "Hold it! Sorry, Emmanuel, but I have to ask: This medicine man, is he a Christian? Or not?"

Emmanuel lowered his voice a notch. "Well, yes, we do have medicine men here who are Christians. But this one here today, I know him and his parents well. And I know he is not a Christian. He thinks you can be a Christian and follow other spirits, because his parents followed other spirits."

"Oh. Okay . . ." The air felt heavy as I thought about it for two seconds. "Well, if the medicine man is not a Christian, then I don't want to see him. Not because I'm afraid of him, because I'm not. But if he really is following other spirits, then those spirits in him will recognize the Holy Spirit in me, and *they* won't want to see me. So what I mean is, if we go to see the medicine man, either: I'm going to do an exorcism, or! I'm going to talk to him about Jesus!"

Emmanuel's voice somehow quickly returned. "Great!! Let's go!" and he spun on his heel and headed into the village.

"Wait!" *What just happened?*

Emmanuel stopped in response to my shout and turned only his head around, as if to say, 'Come on, let's go!'

I stammered, "What I mean is, we can just walk past the medicine man and let him know ahead of time so no one's offended. That's all."

"No! You do not understand!"

He was right—now I was really confused!

Emmanuel turned completely back around to face me directly. "For months, I have been telling these people about the things of heaven, and still the medicine man does not understand! But maybe! if *you* tell him, then he will understand!"

I nodded quickly, simultaneously taking in a breath. Got it. "Okay . . . yeah, I'll do it!"

As we walked toward the medicine man's table, Emmanuel called out in Kinyarwanda to a tall, young man wearing a goatskin. The young man shouted back, Emmanuel gave him a loud, brief response with a chin gesture, and then the young man took off the goatskin.

"What did you tell him?"

"I told him that you do not want to hear about his medicine things—you want to talk to him about Jesus. He said, 'Then can I take off this goatskin?' and I said, 'Sure.'"

Well, that was real.

We stood around the medicine man's table with its clusters of herbs and things—bundles of branches, shrubby stalks, and tightly packed clumps of tiny flowers with twine wrapped around them. Through Emmanuel's translation between us, we talked about what it means to *know* God and to really believe His Word. I shared with the medicine man biblical passages where the LORD makes clear His claim to sovereignty and exclusivity. I quoted Isaiah, the Gospels, Genesis. Through all our back-and-forth discussion, the young medicine man was polite and honest, if not soft-spoken and unmoved.

At some point, he picked up a bundle of herbs and said, "If following other spirits is so bad, then why do people get better when I use these?"

I looked at his face. His eyes were so bloodshot they were red, and his face was expressionless. *Well, LORD, it doesn't seem like we'll be able to break through to him today, but I trust that Your Word never comes back empty, so I'll just let this be planting seeds. I am certain You gave this young man a good mind and that You can bring him to You when the time is right.* In the meantime, I jabbered on for a few more minutes on the ultimate necessity of God being the Creator for the work of truly efficacious healing, the ideological and theological relevance of the salient points concerning this, and an intelligent argument for the overriding supremacy and exclusivity of the Triune God of the Bible—when I suddenly got it. I heard my voice interrupt my thoughts as I realized what the medicine man actually needed from me.

"Wait, are you telling me that God doesn't heal!? Let me tell you some things!" Without hesitation, I recounted to the medicine man the healings I had seen barely a year ago, just across the border in Uganda, in the Kampala government hospital's ovarian oncology ward. "Aminah! Aminah!'" I recalled, with a grateful and joyous smile in my heart to God. Then I launched into sharing about the healing of the Clicks pharmacy staff lady in Gaborone, Botswana. "They begged me to stay and continue to pray for people in the store though I had a bus to catch . . . " For a sliver of a second, I faltered. I wasn't sure if the medicine man or Emmanuel had noticed, but they were graciously still listening to me regardless. Perhaps it was naïve of me not to expect this, but revisiting the memory of my time in Gaborone suddenly brought to mind the deep sadness of my second day there. Throughout that second day at Clicks, I had tried to encourage the staff to pray to the LORD themselves, but the people did the opposite and depended more on me than on the LORD and the fact of His desire to have a relationship with them. It had left me with the persistent, haunting question of what could have been done to prevent that misdirection, and I wondered if I should continue telling the young medicine man all that had happened in Gaborone.

In a brief moment of uncanny timing, the medicine man glanced up and then, with a subtle nod of his head, politely interrupted me as he discreetly pointed to the King's House, a stone's throw behind me. "I see that another visitor is about to come this way. Let us go into this other house and talk more there." And then the medicine man calmly yet immediately turned and walked into the closest house—basically a hut—with Emmanuel in complete sync with him. Feeling clueless, but trusting them and knowing that Theodore was keeping vigilance from where he was resting on the bench in the performance area, I followed along. Close behind us followed one of the musicians whom I had noticed out of the corner of my eye standing nearby during the medicine man's and my discussion. Swiftly but discreetly, this silent, stocky figure joined us.

We entered a compact, round, very neatly-made, mud-covered hut with a generous thatched roof. As the medicine man pulled back the curtain that comprised the entrance to the house, my eyes grew wide with admiration at my surroundings. The hut had appeared to be small on the outside, but it felt larger on the inside—there were two well-dressed, raised beds, a comfortable sitting area, chairs, and a desk, all attractively made with locally sourced wood and grasses. Somehow there was also enough space to allow a safety zone around the pale-colored brick firepit in the middle. A clay vent at the top of the hut permitted smoke to escape (on this occasion the opening was covered, since we did not need a fire), while down below, several neatly woven straw mats covered a thick layer of dried grasses, itself likely covering a mixture of dried manure and mud for the floor. Using the resources of their natural environment, the local villagers had followed traditional techniques and made an immaculate dwelling. Emmanuel quickly explained to me that this hut doubled as sleeping accommodations for tourists by night and as an office space for the cultural community center by day.

Without any further speaking or direction, the four of us stepped into the hut and stood around the four sides of the square-shaped firepit. As soon as we were settled, the musician quietly raised a finger and then said something.

I implored Emmanuel, "What does that mean?"

"He wants to confess his sins."

"Oh—I'm—not a priest!" I apologized to the musician. "But as a sister and as brothers, we can *support* you in your confessing to the LORD."

The musician decided this was good enough, and shared his confession.

As soon as he was done, the medicine man raised a finger and said something. Again, I appealed to Emmanuel.

"He wants to confess his sins too."

And so the medicine man did. He confessed his sins, including that of following other spirits—and renounced his practice of that! I was quietly in awe at the spiritual work of God I was witnessing at that moment, and I thanked Him in the depths of my heart for the privilege of being there.

Then the musician and the medicine man said something to Emmanuel, who explained to me, "Now they want you to pray for them." Ah, an absolution. *Well, I'm neither a priest nor Catholic, but I do appreciate the concept of absolution.* For this culture, I thought it was best for a spiritual leader from within their own community to pray a sort of absolution for them. And, of course, he was standing right next to me, though he didn't know it yet.

"Okay," I responded, "though it won't be an actual Catholic absolution. We'll just pray to affirm that they've been forgiven. . . . So: You lead, Emmanuel, and I'll back you up!"

THE OUTSKIRTS OF MUSANZE

Emmanuel drew a deep breath and straightened his stance. Answering the call to duty, he prayed for his two countrymen in Kinyarwanda. I followed up by praying blessings for each of them.

"Is there a particular worship song in Kinyarwanda . . . ?" I asked.

"Yes! One moment . . . " Emmanuel quickly disappeared for two seconds on the other side of the curtain while it flapped behind him, then reemerged waving a black book in his hand.

"This is a hymnal, though I apologize—it is only in Kinyarwanda. I always keep it at the office desk when it is not in use."

I did a cursory study of the print. "Hey, this is great! I don't understand exactly what the words are saying, but I can follow along and get the spirit of it."

"Yes!" Emmanuel responded. With raised eyebrows, we promptly checked with the young medicine man and the musician, and they were smiling and motioning encouragingly. The four of us crowded around the hymnal and sang praises to God together!

"I must tell you something," Emmanuel said emphatically. "I have been here for seven years. Seven years!! And never, not once, has a tourist offered to pray for us! Until now. Seven years! This is a big thing!"

"Do people in the cultural village pray on their own? And with each other?"

"Yes! For the past five months, I have had a worship service every day after work for a half hour. We pray and worship to heaven. Most of the people here come. The rest of the people from the surrounding villages are not allowed to observe during normal working hours, but I let them watch over the wall when we pray. But never has a tourist offered to pray for us until this day! This is very remarkable!"

The curtain pulled back and Theodore's head appeared in the doorway.

"Is everything okay? What's going on in here?"

Our attention was suddenly flung in the direction of the doorway, where the outline of my driver was surrounded by sunlight streaming in. "Ah, it is good to have some light in here! It was getting dark!" Emmanuel buoyantly greeted Theodore.

"Everything's okay! We've just been—praying," I explained awkwardly.

"Oh-kay . . . ?" More confused than ever, Theodore searched our faces, making sure we were all well.

Behind Theodore, there were flashes of pale grassy headdresses and bold-colored fabrics whipping through the air to the earthy, thunderous rhythm of drumbeats, reedy horns, and hundreds of tinkling bells as the dancers stomped their feet. A traditional wedding dance was on full display in the middle of the cultural village, so we exited, and I sat on the bench and enjoyed the show. Afterward, the other visitors said goodbye and were rushed off with their various drivers to the lodge, while the cultural center staff gathered themselves to form an audience for the goat-gifting ceremony in which I was to participate. Simply put, I would give the goat to a widow from one of the surrounding villages, then be on my way to catch the end of dinner like the rest of the visitors. But in the meantime, to accomplish all this, there was much shifting around of people and objects in various directions, so I stayed off to the side and waited for the convivial commotion to settle. It was at this time that I noticed that, interestingly, it was the medicine man who was set to untie the goat and bring it to me.

Eventually, I was beckoned forward and, unsure of where or how to be for the goat-gifting ceremony, I followed the directions of the staff as they pointed me this way and that for where to greet the widow, where to collect the goat, and finally, where to stand to gift the goat. At the point of collection, when the medicine man held out the goat's rope to me, I grasped the cord then looked up at him. I nearly gasped. The young man's physiognomy had suddenly changed—the redness in his eyes was gone! He was beaming! For a moment, I couldn't move—I was transfixed (honestly, shocked) by so much peace and happiness on his face. Such a transformation! I wondered if anyone else noticed it, but I quickly decided not to say anything to respect the privacy of the medicine man. If others noticed, cool; if not, then maybe it was just for me and God to witness.

Soon enough, the goat ceremony was done. The widow had her new goat, the people were still standing in the middle of the cultural village, I was still standing in front of them, and we were all waiting for Emmanuel to tell us what to do next.

"Well, now . . . " Emmanuel diverted his eyes downward, thinking and consulting his watch. "That concludes the goat ceremony. It is 5:20, and now we will have our program."

Program? What program? Was I supposed to still stand there in front of everyone? "Emmanuel," I hissed, "what program?"

"The one I told you earlier about." I still didn't get it. "You can stay up here or sit down if you like. I am going to give the people a sermon."

Ahhh, it's past closing time and they are overdue for their post-work time of worship. I gladly moved to the sidelines and sat on the bench. I leaned over to Theodore and whispered, "So, uh, tourists sticking around for the worship service—is this normal?" Theodore was staring at the scene in front of him with basket-sized eyes and listening to Emmanuel intently, shaking his head incredulously. "No, this has never happened!"

I relaxed and thought it was a cool privilege to see this intimate time of community worship, even though I didn't understand Kinyarwanda. I wondered if Emmanuel would say anything about the medicine man. To my ignorant ears, it all sounded like elegant murmurs and burbles. *Mm-burble. Mu-burble. Ka-burble.* "Mary." *Uh oh.* And again, *Mm-burble* "Mary." Then Emmanuel started acting out a scene that I realized was of the healings in the Ugandan hospital, followed by that of the Botswana Clicks revival. I shifted my weight on the wooden bench and felt its smoothed grain under my hands as I gripped its edge. In that moment, echoes arose in me of my lingering, pained question from the Gaborone revival—namely, why did the people depend more on me instead of the LORD by the time I left? *I've gotta downplay what's happened here as much as possible,* I thought, with slightly heightening concern.

Meanwhile, the community had broken out into singing and worship to the LORD for what He had done. I got up and, with the aid of Emmanuel's hymnal, joined them for a Rwandan hymn.

Then Emmanuel asked me to pray.

I paused. "How 'bout *you* pray, and I'll follow up?"

Emmanuel gave me a quick nod. "Okay!"

And so we did. It was a great gift to pray with a group of Rwandan Christians, and it was also really cool to pray to the LORD with this group in the center of a wide, open space surrounded by close-knit villages, lush montane forest, the heart-catching Virunga Mountains, and an expansive, cloud-clung sky overhead. With all this and all that had happened, it was a double joy to pray . . . even as I was admittedly planning my escape for as soon as it would be over.

I said a fast goodbye to everyone and apologized for needing to rush back to the lodge. Making concerned eye contact with Theodore (who knew we were *way* beyond the agreed upon half hour), I hurried toward the entrance. Theodore sprang up to accompany me, but it was too late. A dignified and older ex-poacher, who still had the strength and stature to be one of the cultural village's fine traditional dancers, leapt in front of me and dropped to his knees as he made the sign of the cross and bowed his head.

"Oh! You don't need me!" I protested, trying to encourage him to stand. "And I'm not a priest!"

He peered at me with big eyes and a wrinkled brow, then shook his head with an innocent, well-meaning smile.

"Do you understand English?"

Same response, which was response enough.

I decided to give him a friend's blessing and prayer that were admittedly nearly as swift as the breezes I felt as people raced past me to line up behind him. It broke my heart. Some of the people were evidently former poachers and tribal warrior types, and here they were, so very humbly asking for prayer. I didn't want to repeat what had happened in Botswana, but I did not know how to avoid that. The only thing I could think to do, as a sister and friend, was to bless people—for they deserved to know they were loved and blessed by the LORD—and to get out of there as soon as possible. I prayed for the people as fast as my hands and feet could take me and my heart allowed. Then Emmanuel came alongside me to accompany me and Theodore to the exit, which the small crowd deferred to. I did not want to ignore the stream of very beautiful people that had gathered around us and followed us out, but I did not want them to attach too much to me and not enough to God.

Emmanuel, Theodore, and I stepped out of the cultural village with a remarkably quiet crowd right behind and beside us, listening to our conversation as we negotiated our way over the rocky path. Intently, we necessarily focused our discussion on the importance of following up God's miraculous interventions with longer-term discipleship within the community and body of Christ. Soon I estimated that no one had attempted for the past thirty seconds to stop us to have me pray, so I began to relax and figured we were in the clear.

And then I looked up. There was an old man waiting by the side of the road for us. In that moment, there were a lot of people walking with us, but somehow my attention was caught by this elderly gentleman, and once I saw him, it was impossible to un-see him for two reasons. One, he was the most desperate-looking person I had seen in that area. Standing where the dirt path to his little house met the rocky path that we were trudging on, he leaned on a blunt, rugged stick for support, while his clothes were ragged and dirty. Secondly, as soon as I saw him, he made eye contact with me, did the sign of the cross, and pointed to his knee, bound roughly by bandages.

As soon as he did that, I had a feeling in my belly, almost like a punch that didn't hurt, and I heard the LORD say, "This is *it*."

Now?? You want to do this now?? But what about what happened in Botswana? I'm trying to get away—and then I felt this *compassion* for the old man that I knew wasn't from me. It was like God was saying, 'Look at this old man. He is so poor, physically broken, and has humbled himself to ask for help. He hardly has a chance of getting adequate medical care, let alone expert attention in a good hospital. But I love him and want him healed just as much as anyone who has access to medical help. I care for him dearly, so let's do this!'

And with all that, instantly a merciful and wonderful thing happened—suddenly, the focus shifted from me to the LORD's compassion for this old man. The difficulty of what had happened in Botswana was still there, but it ceased to control the situation. Instead, the LORD's love took over. It didn't make sense in my head for *me* to pray for this old man, but I knew that the LORD desperately and powerfully wanted him prayed for and healed. I couldn't figure out what else to do, so I literally took the next step and walked over to the old man, knelt down before him, reached out my hand as I was about to pray aloud for him . . .

Stop! I knew what to do! Still kneeling on the ground, I threw my hands behind my back and called out, "Wait!—Emmanuel! Come here!"

Emmanuel soon appeared next to me and bent down. "Yes?"

I paused for a split second as I chose my words carefully, never taking my eyes off the old man's knee. "I *need* you to pray for healing for this gentleman." I couldn't risk saying 'I *want* you to pray'—it needed to be Emmanuel!

Slightly embarrassed, Emmanuel scooted himself closer and said, "I don't know how to."

"That's all right! I'll guide you!"

I simply walked Emmanuel through what I'd naturally do if I was praying for the old man. I didn't have a formula I could give him, and I realized that what I told Emmanuel to do was so short and simple that he might not believe his prayer to God was effective.

So, when Emmanuel withdrew his hand, we asked the old man if he could tell a difference.

In Kinyarwanda, the knee-weary gentleman said something.

"What did he say?" I asked Emmanuel.

Emmanuel dipped his head down toward me and relayed, "He said, 'Yes!'"

We asked him if it was a lot, a little, or some.

"Some."

Better or worse?

"Better!!"

Can we pray for you again?

I raised my eyes to see the old man's face as Emmanuel translated, and he was shaking it up and down with great enthusiasm!

"Okay, okay! Got it!" I said to the gentleman as I laughed. Emmanuel, of course, naturally translated that as well, and the suspense in the crowd was momentarily broken by their laughter joining mine.

There was a half-second of hallowed hesitation as I, excited at the movement of the LORD, waited for Emmanuel to charge forward, while Emmanuel, reverently concerned to follow instructions exactly, waited for me to tell him what to do next. Again, I led Emmanuel in a very simple prayer and command to the pain and the knee. I watched the knee as Emmanuel prayed and commanded, and this time I saw something strange and remarkable occur. It was as if the stiff knee suddenly became gelatinous, even through the layers of bandages. It immediately seemed ready to wiggle in any direction, and I swung my head up to address the old man and ask him if he could tell any difference.

His countenance said it all! The simultaneous expression of awe, wonder, delight, and joy in the old man's now-beaming face was like that of the young medicine man when he renounced other spirits and committed himself entirely to Jesus as Lord! I heard the words coming out of my mouth, "Ask him where the level of pain is at now, on a scale of . . . " but I knew that they were unnecessary. As it was, those words never got translated or even finished, because just as I began speaking, the old man threw down his stick behind him, turned around, and walk-jogged up and down the dirt path!

The crowd erupted! A great roar of cheering and praising God instantly arose from the people, and before Emmanuel and I could go anywhere, the masses sucked in around us, and immediately a man pushed his way to the middle of the now very large crowd and also pointed to his knee.

"Okay, wait!!" *Good Lord, what do I do?* All I knew was that I didn't want to be the one to pray. The problem I had had in Botswana was partially solved, but not entirely yet, as the crowd reached a level of near-hysteria that I had never personally seen before. I was somehow conscious that we needed someone who was unseen, but who had faith and love for the LORD. I didn't qualify anymore; Emmanuel didn't qualify anymore; we needed someone who was indisputably "the least of these." *We need . . . the old man!*

"Where's the man who's just been healed?" I called out. Frantic searching among the crowd. The old man had sought the LORD, had been loved by the LORD, and had been made the center of a revival in that community. But soon enough, the crowd forgot and had pushed him out of the center. Yet that old man was not to be forgotten. "Where is he?" I repeated, scanning the mass of people.

The old man returned—walking quite fine—with an embarrassed grin on his face from all the attention as the people jostled him back to the center of the crowd.

I told the old man in front of all the people, "You've been healed, so now you have faith. *You* are going to pray, and Jesus is going to heal this man's knee!"

I coached him as I had with Emmanuel, and Emmanuel translated between us. The second man got healed! More cheers and praise to God from the crowd, even as yet another man pressed his way to the center, pointing joyfully and expectantly to his back. So I took the second healed man and taught him to pray and call for healing for the third man, and so forth. This went on for at least five men in a row! The women were not as aggressive as their men, but they shouted out for prayers for their children and babies, which we honored. We also sometimes called out for children who loved Jesus to come and pray for healing for the adults, and the effects were the same.

As for me, well, it was terrific! Apart from praying for babies, I intentionally didn't pray directly for anyone. The LORD knows, I couldn't have been happier—the villagers really did do it all themselves! At the same time, it was an absolute joy and fantastic privilege to be able to coach the villagers in finding this new aspect of their connection with the LORD, something that they had probably received a long time ago, yet hadn't realized.

It also gave me a glimpse of what our Lord might have experienced when he loved and ministered to the crowds as he navigated the best way to serve and be with them. At one point, I was coaching yet another person and we were crouching on the ground to attend to a lower leg injury. As we were doing this, I remember being struck by how quickly it had become nighttime as we worked in the darkness. When we were done healing the person's leg, I looked up so that I wouldn't knock into anyone as I regained a standing position . . . and that's when I saw a circle of blue overhead. Oh my goodness, the crowd had become so dense that they blocked out the sunlight and I thought it was nighttime! And so we continued to joyfully work, and to train, and to celebrate, and to give thanks and praise, and to be healed! We continued until it really did get so dark that I only knew it was Emmanuel standing next to me because I recognized his voice and he spoke English.

"Well, I guess this is enough for today," he said. The people, now noble shadows against the dwindling light of the darkening sky, respected Emmanuel and spread out to give us some space. As they moved, I saw the first few stars of night that had been hiding behind them.

Emmanuel was quite right, and I smiled at his understatement, though probably no one could see it. "Yes, I think so," I replied.

For all of us, there was a moment of shared quiet, a community pause. It felt like we were together taking in, for just a breath, the magnitude and significance of what had happened for us that day. And it left me with the question: How do you close an experience like that?

The people knew the answer, and some women and men called out in Kinyarwanda.

"The people are asking you to close us in prayer," translated Emmanuel.

"Sooooo . . . " I began.

"I'll do it!" answered Emmanuel.

"And I'll follow you up!"

And so we prayed, with so much gratitude and joy. It was such a tremendous and profound gift, to be a part of giving that prayer from the depths of ourselves. The prayer was not long, but respectful, genuine, worshipful, and real. And then it was all over. Or almost.

More voices called out. I couldn't even guess what they would ask this time.

"The people want to know what to call you," Emmanuel appealed to me.

I blinked in thought. But I was not panicked, nor worried any longer about the "Botswana problem." We had overcome it. Perhaps most importantly in this case, I had overcome it.

I figured they were probably expecting something like "Prophet Mary" or "Pastor" or "Bishop." I was glad that the darkness hid my bashful smile, so that it would not be interpreted the wrong way. "Mary.... They can call me 'Mary.'"

The people dispersed a little further so we could proceed down the rugged footpath. Theodore, who earlier had been pushed out to the periphery of the growing crowd during the old man's healing, reappeared and offered to take Emmanuel home—it would give us a chance to debrief and for me to give Emmanuel some suggestions for following up such a remarkable movement of God among the people. As we walked along the path, I noticed that Emmanuel and I were again the only ones talking aloud. There were many people walking with us, however, listening in and moving like ghosts, not wanting to disturb our conversation. As we neared the lights of the clearing, I happened to take a glance back and was astonished by the mass of people following behind us. They had been so quiet and deferential to us that I hadn't realized so many were there. It was very, very humbling, and at the same time, I instantly thought of the Gospel accounts. *Lord, is this what it was like when you were teaching and doing ministry here on earth? Wow!*

The people accompanied us all the way to Theodore's jeep, graciously not saying anything but respecting the conversation I was having with Emmanuel as I tried to explain and advise him as much as I could in a short amount of time. We got into the vehicle and were about to close the doors when I looked at the people one last time, grateful that there was a light by the jeep so I could see their faces and they could see mine. Everyone broke the silence at once, and we all smiled, waving wildly and calling out goodbye many times to each other, even as the jeep barreled down the rocky street.

This was not yet the time to grieve saying goodbye, however. Though I was suddenly feeling my physical tiredness and hunger quickly return, I decided I could block it out for another ten minutes. Time was short! I spun around in my car seat.

"Emmanuel!"

"Yes?"

"Discipleship!"

"Yes, discipleship!"

"Miracles are easy; discipleship is work. But you must do discipleship or connect the young medicine man with a seasoned, born-again Christian who perhaps is also a medicine man, to mentor him. Do you have a local pastor? Can you connect him with a good, solid church?" And so forth. It was a fast ten minutes of discussion and preparation of support for the young medicine man in the wake of his new-found freedom. And then we were at the lodge.

Theodore accompanied me into the lobby and asked to speak to the manager. "You should have been given a bag lunch today, and you must eat!" he had said. "I am going in to make sure they give you what you paid for." When the receptionist left to find the manager and a hot meal for me, Theodore turned to me. I was already on the ground pulling off my dirty hiking boots for the cleaning line.

"I want to thank you for what you did for the community today," he began, his face genuine and humble. "I know these people very well, and believe me, they will not forget what happened today for many years to come!"

The corners of my mouth went up in gratitude. Theodore couldn't have given me a better gift. "Aw. Thanks!"

"Gorilla trekking—that was great! That was fantastic!" He continued, "But tonight?—That was *awesome!!* That was amazing!!!"

I totally agreed! "Theodore," I asked, "so what did Emmanuel say when he was preaching after work hours at the cultural village?"

"Oh, he was talking about what you had said about the healings at the hospital in Uganda, and how you saw God at work in Botswana."

Hmm. Thought so.

"And then he talked about what happened with the young medicine man and how he came to Jesus. He said, 'You can see for yourselves how he has physically changed!'"

Whoa! Now *that* was totally cool!! I remembered that in African villages, people know the members of their community very well, often for life and even beyond—families usually continue in the same village or region for many generations. The value for community is extremely strong, such that when an individual gets touched by the LORD and changes his or her life, their community knows if it is genuine and the extent to which the person has changed. If it was evident to the villagers that the medicine man had changed, then he really had changed! Not that we needed yet more evidence of it by that point. So many wonderful, amazing, glorious things happened that night, and it all began because a young man broke his family's cycle of following other spirits and committed himself fully to Jesus. Such a beautiful, simple, life-changing, community-altering, remarkable event!!

THE OUTSKIRTS OF MUSANZE

A hot meal in a bag arrived for me. I was so ready just to eat and crash, so I bid Theodore adieu for the night. Tired, but overjoyed, I walked back home to my cabin under the light of the moon.

11

Mom

WITH A FISTFUL OF slim sticky note tags in one hand and a mechanical pencil and pen in the other, I glanced up from my Bible as I balanced a stack of open Proverbs commentaries and a course syllabus draft on my lap. I had returned from Rwanda barely two weeks earlier—dusty, tired, and elated—and was now back in the thick of Sacramento life at home, whether it was tending to my mother, weak in health and grieving the loss of Grandma, or putting the final touches on my syllabus for sessional teaching at Eston College. In just three days, I would be back in Canada, catching up with friends at Eston and teaching at my favorite prairie Bible college. All that to say, it was this unusual mix of circumstances that accounted for why I had commandeered a hospital lounge coffee table with my laptop, Proverbs research, and scattered pages of notes as I waited for Mom to return from her routine cardiology appointment.

I laid my eyes on a slow-moving pair moving towards me at the end of a hallway and grinned. My mom was holding the arm of a nurse for support and chatting cheerfully with her while being led back to the waiting room and me. Her eyes brightened and her smile widened as we made eye contact and she waved to me with her free hand. *How in the world I am blessed with such a pure and childlike-hearted mom I don't know*, I told myself for the ten-thousandth time. *Hers is a heart so grateful and responsive to the grace of God in our lives.* Despite their almost diametrically different personalities, if there was one remarkable thing that Mom and Grandma shared, it was a deeply pure faith and trust in God that, to the unfamiliar eye, could be mistaken for innocence or even naïveté. But the last thing that either lady had was an ignorance of the evils and pains of the world around them; my matriarchs had simply chosen to keep their focus on God through thick and thin. This may have been the only thing my mom inherited from Grandma, who lived and died with barely a cent to her name, and she could not have done better. With such faith and joy emanating from her, it was easy to forget that Mom had been suffering from a debilitating illness—Granulomatosis with polyangiitis—for over twenty-five years.

I swiftly shuffled and gathered my spread of Proverbs research into my backpack, then met my mom and the nurse in the hallway.

"Hello!" called out Mom happily.

"Hi Mummy!" I answered, then turned anxiously to the nurse. "How'd we do?"

"Oh, she did great! Everything is normal."

"Is it?" I responded back quickly and with surprise.

"Yes! We'll see May again in four months."

I looked at my mom. "Mummy, did you ask your doctor or nurse?"

"Oh! I forgot!" Mom said with a slightly embarrassed but well-humored laugh.

I addressed the kind nurse again. "My mom's been unusually forgetful this past month. My grandmother—May's mom—passed away about a month and a half ago, so we assumed it was grief-related, but Mom and I agreed that we should ask you."

"Some forgetfulness is very normal in hard grief. I didn't notice anything unusual," said the nurse, smiling at my sweet Mom.

"Nothing we should follow-up or schedule an appointment for?"

"No, she's fine."

"Okay," I nodded. "Thank you."

Mom took my arm and said goodbye to the nurse as I turned us toward the hospital entrance. "Mom, would it be okay if we take that little parking lot transporter to our car? I don't want to tire your feet."

"Okay."

As if on cue, a golf cart rounded the corner and paused at the waiting lounge. Mom and I settled ourselves in the back, and the transporter rolled on.

"Do I need to use . . . ?" Mom paused, searching for her word.

"Need to use . . . ?" I repeated, trying to figure out what Mom was thinking of.

"Ah! Do I need to put on an umbrella?"

All around me was calm—the meandering ride of the golf cart as it hummed along, the gentle dings of a nearby elevator, the soft sunlight suffusing the hospital entrance we were about to exit through, and especially Mom's demeanor as she burrowed lightheartedly along the back seat for her mystery object—all was calm. But I had freezing electricity firing through me! I was terrified! This was beyond my mom having a forgetful moment. To keep her from panicking, I willed to hide my utter fear. Perhaps overcompensating for my rising concern, I reduced my voice to a near-whisper as I responded, "Sorry, what did you say?"

"Ah!" Mom suddenly found what she had been on the hunt for in the golf cart. "Do I need to put this on?" She held up a seat belt.

"Yes, it's a good idea. Here, I'll help you," I offered, keeping my eyes on the seat belt and hoping to distract my mom from my face awhile longer while I absorbed the impact of what had just happened. Meanwhile, we were entering the parking lot, and I hoped that the driver had not heard the details of what my mom had said so as to not alarm her.

"Thank you," said Mom.

"You're welcome, Mummy." I murmured in response, though inside my brain was on overdrive.

Still willing myself to stay calm enough to sound reasonably relaxed, I said, "Hey, Mummy, would it be okay if I just—do a little test?"

Mom nodded.

I held up the seat belt next to me. "What do you call this?"

"An umbrella."

"You sure?"

"Uh-huh."

"What's it used for?"

"To . . . buckle yourself in," she said, making fastening actions.

"Okay, good." This was hard. I wasn't sure what to do.

"Can we get ice cream?"

"Yeah," I answered half-absentmindedly, then realized this could be an opportunity to buy more time to probe further before arriving home and risking Mom settling into a deep midday nap. "Let's do that."

The transporter halted to a stop, and the driver called out, "I think this is your section! Do you see your car?"

MOM

"It's right here. Thank you so much!" I unbuckled my mom, and the driver gave her a hand out of the golf cart. At least he apparently hadn't heard our conversation, nor was he giving Mom a reason to panic.

"There ya go," he waved cheerily to my mom and me. "Y'all have a nice day!"

I sat across the faux-marble table from my mom and tried not to appear anxious as I waited for her to finish her double-scoop peach ice cream sundae. Though I knew it wasn't actually the case, it felt like the slowest consumption of ice cream I had ever witnessed. I tried not to speak too much so my mom would finish her dessert sooner, while Mom chatted between spoonfuls, blissfully unaware of my urgent concern.

"Do you think we should bring home a pint for Peter?" Mom asked, referring to our usual tradition.

"Sorry—" Her words shook me back to attention. "Could you repeat that?"

"Should we bring home a pint for Peter?"

"Peter?" I checked that my mom really meant her brother living on the other side of the country instead of her son.

"Yes!"

A small gulp went down my throat. "You mean . . . Ben?"

"Oh! Right!" Mom corrected herself with that sweet and slightly embarrassed smile. "Ben! Not my brother."

"Yes, Ben . . . "

Mom was down to one scoop of her sundae, and I figured time had been ticking long enough. I gently pushed my empty petite ice cream cup to the side, felt another gulp slide down my throat, folded my hands together on the table, exhaled, and as collectedly as possible said, "Hey, Mom?"

Mummy looked up, her ice cream spoon still in her hand. "Uh-huh?"

"So uhh, you remember when we were in the golf cart in the parking lot earlier?"

"Yeah."

"Do you . . . remember saying that an umbrella is a seat belt?"

"No."

I drew in a deep breath, thinking. "Okay . . . " I continued, trying to keep my voice cool and matter-of-fact sounding instead of condemnatory, "Well . . . you did say that." Watching her face carefully, I proceeded, "You know—how—you said just now your brother's name instead of Ben's?"

"Mm-hm."

"Well, I know these kind of things happen sometimes, but it seems to be happening an unusual amount now."

"Yeah."

Did Mom say, Yeah? I decided to cut to the chase, but still forced an air of nonchalance for her sake. "Would it be okay if—we just—swing by Urgent Care? Pop in, get it checked out?"

"Yeah."

"Not to panic. I'm just being overly careful."

Mom nodded.

"No rush. We'll wait 'til you finish your ice cream," I said with a weak smile. "But maybe we'll skip Ben's pint today."

About an hour later, I was ushered into an examining room at Urgent Care to join my mom and the unassuming, but wise elderly doctor there. They were simply sitting in two chairs opposite each other, apparently in conversation. As I approached them, Mummy was silent but looked up at me with goggle eyes—a clear warning in "Mom-speak"—while the doctor held out to me a bright yellow piece of paper.

As I took the piece of paper, he said with a practiced composure that I had to admire, "I'm sending her to ER. She's having a minor stroke. She needs to get there immediately, and she'll get there faster if you drive her instead of me calling and waiting for an ambulance."

Though I could not have imagined those details, Mom's eye-alert communication had already whipped me into hyper-focused attention. I managed to bob my head and queried, "Minor stroke?"

"Yes."

"I can drive fast, but you're sure I'll be faster than an ambulance?"

"Well, don't drive crazy—if you leave now and go straight to ER, you'll be fine. I've given you a Fast Track pass, so once you get there, they'll take care of her immediately." I glanced down at the yellow ER Fast Track pass in my hand, then back up at my mom and the Urgent Care doctor.

"Right—okay—thank you," I managed to say to the doctor as I reached over to help him steady my mom up from the chair. "Okay, Mom, let's go!"

Three hours later, I stood next to a technologist in the control room of an MRI suite, observing my mom and the staff preparing her to be taken through a giant magnet. She could see us through the large glass window, and the technologist would be able to pause the imaging to enable two-way speaker communication with her from within the scanner itself.

"She's about to go in. Want to say anything to her?" he asked in an energetic voice.

"Sure. . . . Hi, Mom! You ready?"

"Hi, Mary! Yes!"

"I know you've done this before. Well, we both have. Pretty simple. You know what to do."

"Yeah!"

"Okay! We'll talk soon—as soon as you're done. Have a good nap!" I half-joked this to my mom, because we both knew that MRIs could take a long time to be completed. Naturally, the easiest way to maintain the necessary stillness during scanning was simply to rest.

The technologist took his finger off the button and announced, "Here we go!"

I stared at the computer screen that was slowly building an image of my mother's brain. After awhile, I turned my gaze to Mom, who seemed to be doing fine. In fact, the technologist chuckled when he pressed the red button to check on her and was met with the sound of snoring. I occupied myself by wandering around the tiny room, reading protocol charts and examining diagrams. As I tried not to be bored, I wondered if it had been a good idea for me to request being in the control room during Mom's long MRI.

"Whoa—" The technologist's reaction drew me back to the computer. He grabbed the mouse and started clicking away, drawing lines on an image of my mom's brain. "What's your mom here for?"

"Um—a minor stroke."

"That's not just a minor stroke. Your mom ain't going home tonight!" he forewarned, leaning towards the screen as he rapidly marked measurements.

"What do you mean?"

"See this mass over here?" He pointed at the screen, though he didn't need to. Unfortunately, it was obvious, even to a minimally trained eye like mine. "That . . . " He shook his head, not able to say the words.

" . . . doesn't belong there," I supplied, my near-frozen voice reduced to a monotone.

"Not at all. . . . And it's big."

"Looks like it. What is it?"

"A mass of some sort. The doctor will have to review the scan and tell you."

"Oh man."

"It's a good thing you got her here when you did. I'm sure she'll get admitted to the main hospital tonight, and they'll operate on it as soon as possible." He paused, still staring at the screen. "Does your family have a history of cancer?"

"No, none at all," I answered quickly. Then my eyes narrowed for few seconds, as I remembered something. "But my mom has had a complicated medical history because of Granulomatosis with polyangiitis."

"What's that?"

"It used to be called Wegener's. It's an autoimmune condition she got when she was exposed to a wallpaper remover that had been taken off the market, but she didn't know it."

"Man . . . "

"Yeah. . . . I remember about twenty years ago she was on an alternative medication for handling menopause with Granulomatosis. She said that medication could shorten her life in twenty years' time, but her doctors were hoping that the medical field would advance enough that they'd have an antidote for it if she needed it." I stared at the MRI. "I wonder if all this is related to that."

"It's an interesting suggestion."

"Yeah. . . . "

"Well, your mom's done, so it's time to get her out of the MRI room. Wanna say anything to her?"

"Yeah, I do." I shook out of my rumination and moved purposely toward the microphone. *LORD, help me. As far as it depends on me, I am not going to let her fall.* "Hi, Mom! You awake?"

"Yeah, though I think I fell asleep for awhile."

"You did. Glad you got a nap. You did good, Mom. I'll see you in a few minutes and we can talk more."

* * *

An hour later, in the dim light of a curtained ER cubicle, while my mom slept, I got out my laptop and wrote a necessary email.

Dear Eston College colleagues,

I'm writing this from the hospital, where I regretfully must cancel the plan for me to teach at Eston next week. We just discovered that my mom has a brain tumor (4 cm!) and her medical situation is currently serious. They are *hoping* to be able to operate soon. At the moment, she is very confused, sometimes agitated, and sometimes tries to do things that she shouldn't, so now is definitely not a good time to leave her. Regarding the Proverbs course, I can propose a few options, and you may think of more. Firstly, . . .

In the meantime, I'll contact the various airlines to cancel my flights. I'm very sorry that I am not able to come at this time and that these are such untimely, difficult, and inconvenient events for us all. While I'd love it if my mom walks out of the hospital totally healed tomorrow, I recognize that the Spirit's manner of work on this one may be beyond my understanding right now. I do know this much: God gave me a mom, and it is one of the highest privileges of my life to be able to care for her at this most difficult time for her.

Every blessing,
Mary

And so, three days later, I was not on a plane bound for Canada. I was lying on a bench in the surgical unit's waiting lounge, trying to catch up on sleep as I waited for my mom's three-hour operation to be completed. Instead, it was seven hours later when I was finally awoken by a nimble hand shaking my shoulder. I started awake at the nurse's action, grabbed my eyeglasses, and sat up.

"Your mother's surgery is complete, and she's now in Post-Op resting. You can see her in a few minutes."

I took a deep breath. "Thank you. How does it look?"

"The surgeon got it all out, but the biopsy will take several days to come back with results. In the meantime, your mother will go to Acute Rehab to recover as much as possible."

"Is there a prognosis?"

"The doctor will be able to discuss that with you."

"Okay . . . do you usually see people with tumors this big recover?"

Having mercy on my desperation, the nurse said, "We do, with further therapy."

"Further therapy . . . "

"Chemotherapy. Radiation therapy. Physical therapy. Probably some speech therapy . . . Does she have help at home?"

"She does." Or rather, as I was thinking, *She does now!* "Me. . . . Probably my brother, too."

"Good. She'll need that."

"Which way to Post-Op?"

"Down that hall, and to the left. Follow the signs for the Recovery Room. It's not a fancy hotel, but she's comfortable—we've got her on a lot of painkiller for now."

I wish I could get Mom to a fancy hotel—anywhere far from this nightmare! I rose from the bench and shook the sleep out of my legs. *But it will probably be a very lengthy time before I can take her anywhere.*

"Thanks," I managed to say to the nurse. It was genuine—even through my grief, I was grateful for medical resources. And then I headed toward the hallway, my eyes focused ahead. *Oh Mummy, this is going to be a long journey. God help us, we'll do our best.*

12

Miki

"Gilbert!" I shouted, running across the street to the familiar grassy mound on a sun-splashed afternoon. "What is that?!"

Our neighbor Gilbert, a convivial combination of kindness, compassion, bird rehabilitation, and wine-sipping, held up a Labrador Pit Bull puppy he had recently rescued. Evidently he had decided to expand his aid beyond feathered friends. "We've been rehabilitating him these past few days. I've already got a new forever home lined up for him!" Gilbert lowered the little brown mass and with one hand held him out to me. "Isn't he so cute!"

I took him into my hands. "He's so light!"

"We've already got two of our own, but I wish we could keep him!"

"We've never had a dog, but I wish we could keep him, too." I peered at the puppy's tiny face as he wiggled in my hands. "Everyone's been telling me I should get a little dog for my mom. Even her rheumatologist recommended it! I seem to be the only one who thinks that would be a bad idea."

"Whoa, what do you mean? Dogs are great!" protested my animal-loving friend.

"I'm sure they are, but they seem to need a lot of care and maintenance. For the average person, that's okay. But, for my mom, who in the past five years has been through brain surgery, acute rehab, chemo, radiation therapy, more chemo, more radiation, and a series of strokes, it would be taking too many risks." I saw that Gilbert was tracking with me, so I continued, "I maintain as sterile an environment around her as possible.

So would I have to clean the dog every time he gets on her hospital bed? Would it get along with her carers? Ben moved to Oklahoma for a job, so Mom needs my attention now more than ever. I don't have time to take care of a dog like it would deserve."

"Awww, well that's okay. You're doing exactly what you need to right now. You can always come here and borrow our dogs when you need some doggy cuddle time."

"Thanks, Gilbert," I said with a grateful smile. "Would it be okay if I show this little guy to my mom? Just to see if she might respond to a dog well? Maybe I could bring doggy visitors to her every once in awhile."

"Sure!"

"Okay, I'll be right back with this little one."

"Mummy!" I exclaimed as I entered the family room, where her hospital bed was now situated to give her a view of her garden. "Gilbert rescued a puppy! Want to see the cute puppy?"

Mom rolled over in her bed and eagerly turned towards the mystery object. I held out the limp, somnolent pup in my hands. Her eyes fluttered, then ballooned wide with surprise.

"Want to keep him?" I tested.

Mom shook her head.

"Really?" I checked her response. "No?"

She shook her head again, clearly.

I cradled the near-sleeping puppy in my arms and said to him, "Don't worry, little guy, you're still loved!" *Oh man, Mom, as Grandma would say: Picky picky!* I hurried the sweet canine out of the room and back to Gilbert, thinking that if I were ever to get my mom a dog, it would be challenging! In truth, I actually did know what kind of dog my mom wished for. She had been telling me so all my life. Even now, as a trach prevented her from speaking, she was still telling me that, albeit with her eyes instead of her mouth. *How in the world will I find her a white Lhasa Apso?*

I had done a cursory scan online once, out of curiosity, and discovered that Lhasa Apso puppies cost hundreds of dollars! If we sought Lhasa Apsos available for adoption, the only place in Northern California with any was the Bay Area (at the time, there were a total of just one or two), and that destination was too hectic for my mom to travel to in her very fragile condition. On top of all this, again, did I really want the added risks and responsibility of dog ownership in the same sphere as caring for my beloved mom in her dependent state?

But after that day with Gilbert's rescue puppy, when I had a spare moment (which was super rare) or needed a brain break (not rare at all), I would do a Northern California–wide online search for Lhasa Apsos available for adoption. Late one night, I found a brown Lhasa Apso that would be available for meet-and-greets at a pet shop in Stockton on a Saturday. Mom was too tired that Saturday to journey to Stockton, so I planned our trip to see the little brown dog the next weekend. Little brown dog was snagged within three days, however, by a wise and more ready forever home. *LORD God, I know this isn't really vital for Mom's living, but I would really like to bless her heart with the dog of her dreams—something that isn't just about survival, but about the things that make life worth living. If this pleases You, would You lead me to the right dog in a short time? But only as You know best, Lord!* I resumed my occasional search for an adoptable white Lhasa Apso in Northern California, despite not knowing anything about dogs and having my misgivings about assuming responsibility for one. In truth, I was driven by my mother's loneliness—I and her carers were there, and a handful of precious and faithful friends from the Moms Prayer Group visited regularly. Yet as great a blessing as they were, I saw that she still missed many of her friends and family and just having someone more present who could engage her and love her and give her hugs or snuggles. So, it did not take long for me to see and accept that maybe it was time to find that white Lhasa Apso! To avoid disappointing my mom in case my pursuit were to prove futile, I kept my quest a secret until I might find that elusive unicorn of a dog.

A couple weeks later, as I sat in the dark on the floor next to my mom's hospital bed, I scrolled through a dog rehoming site and came across a photo of a scruffy, white-haired, elderly Lhasa Apso. He was in Yuba City, just over an hour away. I could hardly wait for daylight. As early as it was reasonable to call in the morning, I got on the phone. An older gentleman, Stanley, answered. He had already received a couple requests for his sweet dog but hadn't been convinced that those would-be homes would give "Mickey" the stability and support he needed. Mickey needed a human who would be especially present, not carting him off to the workplace everyday or confused about which cheap can of dog food to feed him.

"Well, my mom had a stroke and is in a dependent state, so she's home nearly all the time, and someone is always with her. I can guarantee that Mickey will always have at least human company and healthy food."

"This sounds good. I actually have a disability, and Mickey has been great at keeping me company when I've had to stay home. He's a great dog! If my wife didn't want to breed Chihuahuas, I would for sure keep him. For sure!"

What if I'm wrong? What if he bites or stays away from Mom? "Can we meet him? It would be good to see how he and my mom get along."

"Yes. When were you thinking?"

"As soon as possible." If this dog was a match for my mom and we had a chance to adopt him, I didn't want to miss it. However, Easter weekend was coming up and not even the prospect of the ideal dog could draw us away from prayers and celebrations at church.

"Tomorrow okay?"

"We'll take it!"

I got off the phone and ran to my mom's hospital bed in the family room. Her carer Ruthie had just finished feeding Mom her mid-morning snack. "Mom!! We've got to pray! I might have found your dog!"

"Whaaaat?" Ruthie shot me a befuddled expression as she closed the port on Mom's feeding tube. "Did you say your family has a dog?!"

"No! But we might in the near future—the very near future! I've been searching for months for my mom's dream dog, and I think he's in Yuba City. Can you come with us tomorrow to help my mom meet him? I'm hoping to figure out if they're a match before Easter weekend."

"Oooh yes, I love dogs! How does that sound, Mrs. May? Would you like a dog?"

"It's a white Lhasa Apso, to be exact!" I hastily added before my mom might protest.

Mom turned her head toward us. The corners of her mouth curled up. And she blinked enthusiastically. That was more than enough of a response for me.

We could hardly wait for tomorrow.

The sunshine reflecting off the pavement was near-blinding as Ruthie pushed my mom's wheelchair down the sidewalk and up a driveway into the shade of an open garage. It was a balmy day in Yuba City, but I had a light scarf bundled around my mom's neck to protect her trach and help her not feel self-conscious on this most unusual of outings. In my mind, having protected Mom from the elements and contagious illnesses to the best of my ability and by the grace of God, I was now going to expose her to a dog we knew nothing about except that he was cute and had the outward appearance of the dog of her dreams. I desperately prayed for success and that nothing dangerous would happen to my mom.

Stanley appeared and greeted us all kindly. "Wanna meet him?" he asked, casually kicking a pebble off the driveway.

"Yes, please!" I answered.

"Mic-key!" the man hollered. I did not know where to watch for this near-myth of a dog, then suddenly I caught sight of a happy little bundle of white fur bounding across the front lawn toward Stanley. "There ya go! Good boy!" He simply scooped up the dog, carried him over to my mom sitting in her wheelchair in the garage, and sat Mickey on her lap. Surrounding Mom and Mickey on three sides, Stan, Ruthie, and myself stood there and watched.

Mickey did not move, except to keep panting and smiling in the warm, spring air. Mom took her right arm (her "good" arm) and reached for Mickey's leg. She gently held on to him and showed no signs of letting go. Mom and dog sat there in this manner for quite awhile, and I could only stare. *Is he going to bite her? Will she pull him down? Is he going to jump off?* My astonishment was interrupted by the honk of a nose being blown loudly, and I spun around to see that Stan had hastily grabbed a paper towel and was dabbing his eyes. I peeked back at Mom and Mickey. They were still a calm and content pair. A few moments later, Stanley had regained his composure and returned to my mom's side.

"Looks good. What d'ya think?" Stan asked me, with a sniff.

"I think it's good," I agreed, slowly nodding and still staring at the sweet little spectacle of Mom-plus-Mickey.

"So. You'll take him home with you now."

"Wha—now? Uh—yes! What do you feed him?"

"Whatever's on sale at the warehouse. Three treats before every meal."

"How do you cut his hair?"

"It's thick. Use horse clippers. Got mine on eBay. Want his clothes?"

"Sure. Oh! Medical records?"

"Medical records? Uh, he hardly has any, but I can give them to you. Just his rabies shots. He's up-to-date." Stan left briefly to get Mickey's medical records and a couple sweaters, and I swung back again towards the little dog sitting on my mom's lap, perfectly at ease. *Still no biting, no jumping . . . This is our dog now! Just like that! This little guy has joined our family and it feels like so much is going to change, though I don't know how and I don't feel as ready as I'd like to be. . . . I guess this is how everyone feels when they get a new kind of pet for the first time or are blessed with a child. I hope we'll do this dog good. There's a new creature in our family!*

Stanley returned with a bag and a folder. I, in turn, extended a plastic bag towards him. "I have some gifts for you and your family, but can we also give you something for all the time and care you've given Mickey?"

"I was thinking seventy, but how 'bout half that and donate the rest to Lhasa Apso Rescue?"

"I'll do that."

"Take care of him. You'll be good owners, I can tell," said Stan. He scratched Mickey's fluffy head one more time. "You be a good boy. You're going to a new home now."

With gratitude and respect for Stan's necessary loss that was our gain, we quietly loaded Mom and her new dog into the van. I rolled down the window and waved to Stan until I needed both hands to turn the wheel and round the corner. And so we headed back to Sacramento and home.

Ruthie asked me during this maiden voyage home for Miki, who was sitting on her lap, "Mary, are you going to rename him?"

"I don't think so. I'm not keen on the fact that he was named after a cartoon mouse, but he's used to being called 'Mickey' and I don't want to confuse him. However, I am planning to change the spelling of his name to something cooler and to reflect his Asian background better. I mean, he is a Lhasa Apso."

"Ohhh, Lhasa Apsos are Asian dogs?" Mickey leaned into Ruthie as she scratched his ears.

"Yeah, they originated from Tibet. Though obviously Mickey was born here." I glimpsed sideways at the newest member of our clan as he watched the scenery pass by through the window. "I'm thinking that I'll spell his name M-I-K-I and give him a distinctive middle name. 'Karasimbi'—what do you think of that?"

"Say that again?"

"'Karasimbi.' It's Kinyarwanda for the highest mountain in Rwanda. It means 'little crystals' or 'snow.'"

"Ahhh . . . You're always so thoughtful, Mary, though I think I will opt to call him the shorter name for now!" Ruthie gave Miki's back a couple long strokes, then turned around to address his new owner. "Mrs. May, are you happy you have a dog now? Mi-ki!"

Through the rear view mirror, I saw Mom raise her right arm, then lower it. I could feel the smile on my face and it felt good. "I'm glad you're happy, Mummy!" I called back to her. "Thanks be to God! Can you believe it? He's given you exactly what you wanted, what you've been praying for in your heart all these many years—for decades, even before I was born!" I stole another glance in the rear view mirror as Mom raised and lowered her right arm again. Her face was glowing with happiness!

And that is how, after forty-six years—and three days before Easter—Mom finally got the dog of her dreams, Miki Karasimbi.

13

A Birthday in Yosemite

"Ruthie, can you wake up my mom?" I called out, keeping my eyes glued to the winding road we were following in heavy darkness. "I think we're almost there!"

I heard a mellifluous voice behind me. "Mrs. May? Happy birth-day! Would you like to wake up? Mary says we're almost in Yosemite."

"Actually, we've been in Yosemite for awhile. Sorry, you would have known this if we had arrived during daylight and you could see Half Dome and Bridalveil Falls."

"It's my fault. We would have been on time if I hadn't forgotten to pack your mom's eyeglasses."

"It's okay! We all forget things sometimes. I'm just glad you could come along for this little birthday trip for my mom! Thank you again to your family for letting you be away this long."

"Oh, I want to be here! It's an honor to spend Mrs. May's birthday with her. And I've never really seen Yosemite." I could hear the slight shift in volume as Ruthie respectfully turned towards my mom to address her directly. "This is a gift for me, too, Mrs. May. Thank you! Hap-py Birth-day!"

My eyes twinkled. Ruthie was gold. "Oh! Ruthie, can you please get my mom's eyeglasses on her now? It's time to get ready to move. I'm seeing lights ahead.... I think it's Curry Village."

Balancing Miki—who had fallen asleep on my lap in the new red sweater my mom had selected for him—I steered the minivan down a narrow, curved path, past the iconic saplings-and-lights "Camp Curry" entrance sign, and positioned us into an accessible parking space. I whipped the blue handicapped placard onto the rear view mirror with a *clack*, tightened Mom's old English wool scarf around my neck, and picked up her drowsy dog with one arm as I swung open the driver's door. The sparkling, crisp November air was flush with the comforting, addictive smell of wood-burning fires, and it smacked me delirious in the face before I even stepped out of the van. Heading toward the honeyed-white twinkle lights at Stoneman Cottage, the cozy and rustic motel that we would be overnighting in, it all felt like magic.

I fetched the keys from reception while Ruthie rolled Mom in her wheelchair over crunching conifer needles and dry oak leaves, then up a wooden ramp to a simple, but warm and homey room. We quickly got ourselves settled in, and while Ruthie enjoyed a double bed for herself, I grabbed the Yosemite Guide and snuggled next to my slumbering mom and her lightly snoring dog. As I scanned through the guide's helpful information and schedule of programs, I heard a long, relaxed sigh from the other bed.

"You still awake?" I chided Ruthie, who was gazing up at the ceiling.

"Yes," said Ruthie, thoughtfully. "I just finished saying my prayers. So much to be thankful to God for." Ruthie rolled towards my cozy family, half-hidden behind the open newspaper. "You're reading the Yosemite Guide at this hour? You're not tired?"

"I've gotta plan for tomorrow—we got here late, so we're celebrating Mom's birthday tomorrow, and I don't want to risk delaying it any further. I just saw that there's a free 'Fireplace Storytelling Hour' tomorrow night at the Ahwahnee. My mom would love that! So I'm thinking we'll have a gentle walk and wheelchair push around familiar sights for my mom tomorrow in the morning, let her have lunch and a nap in the afternoon, then take our time getting to the Ahwahnee for dinner in the Café-Bar, followed by the Fireplace Storytelling Hour in the Great Lounge." Despite my excitement, I tried to keep my voice quiet so as to not wake my mom.

Ruthie did the same. "Wowww," she near-whispered. "But what is 'the Ahwahnee'?"

I heard myself take a deep breath. After a couple seconds of thought, I answered, "So ... *the Ahwahnee* is this historic, posh hotel in Yosemite that my mom has always had a fascination with. We've never stayed there, and it was too posh for my dad, who had simpler taste. But one of my earliest memories of Yosemite is of my mom taking my brother and me by the hand into the Ahwahnee lobby and hoping to treat us to an ice cream soda or root beer float in the café-bar. The place was so special to her that she virtually had us tiptoe over the floor mosaics as we entered. She always liked to remind us that at least three U.S. presidents, Judy Garland, and kings and queens like Elizabeth II had stayed there."

"Mary," Ruthie hissed, "we're going there for dinner tomorrow night?!"

"Shhh! Yes! But just to the café-bar, which will be cheaper and more casual. My mom will feel less self-conscious there than in the dining room, which is much fancier. Hopefully they'll let her service dog accompany her, and we can get just a table in a corner of the café-bar and do her tube feeding there. That way, she can legitimately say that she had her birthday dinner in the Ahwahnee!"

Ruthie rolled back to face the ceiling and sighed again. "God is good!"

"He is, Ruthie, He is!"

Not more than two seconds passed by, and Ruthie, staring up again, resumed. "Mary, do you ever miss traveling?"

"You mean like what we're doing right now? Nah, we travel all the time. Remember, we've taken Mom to the Marin Headlands countless times, and I took her to Saratoga twice to see my cousin and attend a Josh Groban concert. This is our first time to Yosemite outside the summer, but our fourth little trip here this year."

"Yes, it's been amazing that you've been able to do all that for your mom. But I mean big travels, like you used to do on your own."

"Oh!" I laughed. "Yeah, I used to travel a decent amount. I don't really miss it, though. I miss a lot of people, so it makes me want to revisit some places in the future, but I'm perfectly content staying home now and just being with my mom. My brother Ben lives far away, and my mom is really the only family I've got left. For the past several years, my life seemed defined by where I was located and what I was doing, but since I came home to help take care of my grandma, life has been . . . richer . . . more fulfilling. . . . I feel—" I searched for the words "—I feel more satisfied. I know some people find that hard to believe, but it's a matter of values and God, really. So yeah, it's been good. It's been work, but it's been good. Totally worth it. As some of us often said in seminary, it's much less about where I am than whom I'm with."

"Hmm, I get that. . . . But if you had the time, where would you revisit?"

I smiled at Ruthie's persistence. "Rwanda. For sure. The people are amazing, and they've been through so much. I could say that about a lot of people and places, but since I had the very great privilege of interacting with the people in Rwanda and seeing God work even through my short visits there, it's a special blessing to catch glimpses of their journey and continued walk with God. I still remember specific people; they remember me; until I needed to really focus my time on Mummy, we were good at staying in touch on email and praying for each other."

"You've been back to visit them, right?"

"Yes, once. At the five-year mark I went on a Compassion International trip to visit the children I had been writing to in Rwanda, and then I squeezed in an unannounced visit to the Cultural Community Center, Emmanuel, and the old man who had been healed and his family—you remember, right? He was the first one to be physically healed. I had also hoped to see my ol' guide and driver, Theodore, and the young medicine man who had renounced other spirits—he was really the one who launched the revival by his internal healing. But since I didn't tell them ahead of time that I was coming, Theodore was off somewhere else doing a tour and the young medicine man was simply not there. He had gotten super serious about being a Christian, thrown himself into church life, and quit the medicine man thing entirely. So it was great! Seriously! If there was anyone I didn't want to see for the best of reasons, it was him—he and his wife were out in their fields instead, because now they are potato farmers."

"Wow. . . . Praise God!"

"Totally. . . . But I'm home now, with Mummy and Miki and you and Auntie Clarinda and Uncle Arnold and our kind neighbors and friends and—most of all—God. I'm so blessed to be able to be here and doing this, and I can see God in it. There's no other place I'd rather be."

"God is good."

"Amen. But Ruthie, how about you? If you could visit anywhere, where would it be?"

"Oh, I would like to see my relatives in the Philippines. I haven't seen my grandmother for years, and I have some uncles, aunts, a lot of cousins . . . But everyone else in my family is here. Even my mother is here. So this is home."

"Yeah. . . . Totally."

"Mm-hmm. . . ."

"Your mom—do you talk to her much?"

"You know, I love her and she can talk—I mean, she has the strength and good health to be able to walk and talk and do what she likes. But your mother—though she cannot talk, I feel closer to her. . . . Your mother talks through her care, her face, her hand, even though she can only use one."

"Well, since the trach was taken out, she can say 'Yes,' 'No,' ' 'kay,' 'Why?' . . ."

" . . . 'Who?' 'Good morning' . . . "

"That one's special for you, Ruthie."

Ruthie grinned broadly.

"But yeah, I know what you mean. I'm very blessed . . . "

I flipped through the last couple pages of the Yosemite Guide and soon heard Ruthie's soft snore join Mom's and Miki's. As I switched off the light and pulled the pinecone-patterned quilt over me, it was a blessing to sense that, somehow, we all knew that Mom's birthday was going to be wonderful.

14

Nate

When one has a dog, an elderly lady in a wheelchair, and an assistant from a tropical climate who has never seen snow, on a frigid November night you don't exactly tiptoe delicately into the Ahwahnee, nor do you pause before entering to whisper reminders to the small and delicately-footed (of which we were none on that day!) about the royalty, world leaders, and celebrities who had graced its halls. Instead, we kept a generously-sized knit hat pulled over Mom's ears, tucked layers of warm blankets around her, hoisted her dog into a doggy frontpack that I wore, and—as Ruthie herself politely but candidly complained of the cold—rushed hurriedly down the red-carpeted, covered walkway, not pausing to admire the Douglas Fir poles or fancy window displays that lined its path.

"I'm so glad its toasty in here! Mummy, can you see the mosaics on the floor? Ah wait, Ruthie, could you please find my mom's eyeglasses?" I asked, as Ruthie rummaged through a small bag hanging on the back of my mom's wheelchair.

"Here, Mrs. May, now you can see the Ahwahnee!"

"Take a quick look, Mom! We've gotta get over to the café-bar in case there's a wait."

Thankfully, there was not a long wait, and Mom and her service dog were especially welcomed to any table that would be comfortable for them. Ruthie and I tucked us all into a corner area, ordered a couple bowls of chili, and enjoyed a relatively relaxing time drinking glass goblets of the truly sweet Yosemite tap water (Ruthie had not believed me until she brushed her teeth the night before) and discreetly syringing a pureed meal of salmon and kale to my mom through her tummy tube. Though I had tried at first to keep us well-paced to arrive on time at the Fireplace Storytelling Hour, it soon became clear that Mom was enjoying her Ahwahnee dinner experience—yes, even without being able to taste any of the Ahwahnee's fare—and that a gentler tempo for the evening would be best for her peace of mind and stomach. So we took our time. We rested. We drank more water. We sat and enjoyed being able to say that we all had dined together in the Ahwahnee for Mom's birthday, regardless of the fact that it wasn't in the actual Dining Room. Close enough, we said. And great enough, too! we said. We took fun pictures. We marveled that Miki was so nicely-behaved there. And after all that, we were ready to move on to the Fireplace Storytelling Hour.

I checked the time. "Oh my goodness! The storytelling hour will be halfway over! Should we still go?"

"I'm open to it," said Ruthie, patting her stomach and welcoming of more time to sit and digest her bellyful of chili.

"We'll need to rush if we're to catch any decent amount of it."

"Okay! Zoom zoom!" Ruthie bounced up and cheerfully spurred us on, grabbing the wheelchair's handlebars.

"Keep your glasses on, Mummy—we'll be going by a lot of cool things quickly. Sorry about that!"

Ruthie pushed Mom's wheelchair down the long hall, while I gave her directions from behind and carried Miki in the frontpack, rubbing his belly so he wouldn't be alarmed at our fast pace. As we neared a corner, I heard a voice speaking—loud and clear, but not harsh; articulate and expert, but not intimidating; engaging and deeply interested, but not aggressive. Oh yes, and he was saying something about trains and Yosemite.

"Ruthie, slow down! We're almost there! Enter quietly!"

And so, finally, we tiptoed into the Great Lounge of the Ahwahnee. Or at least, we tiptoed as much as a lady in a wheelchair, the kind carer pushing her, and her daughter following behind wearing a small white dog can tiptoe.

The speaker was momentarily distracted by us, perhaps intrigued, and he briefly turned his head to look at us. At the same time, I was simply curious to lay eyes on the golden-voiced speaker and the legendary, Behemoth-sized spectacle of a fireplace behind him. So, I turned my head towards him. But somehow, I never really saw the famous fireplace (or much else) in that moment. What I did see was a slender, intense, super intelligent, sensitive, kindhearted, and very, very cute man speaking way over my head about railroad tycoons a century ago. Far from a flamboyant type, he immediately conveyed honesty, integrity, a quiet and solid mastery of and respect for his subject matter, and a natural sweetness. He had stature and a wholesome confidence—but was that fleeting look one of slight nervousness when he caught sight of me?

Suddenly, I felt a punch to my stomach—except it didn't hurt—and it said, "This is it . . . !"

What?!! Wait, no! This is not the time! This is not the place! I've got a mom to take care of! It was a feeling similar to one I had known only once before—on the critical brink of a revival in Rwanda—and yet this one was qualitatively different. If the first one was about power, faith, and healing, this one was about intimacy, commitment, and love.

I refused to look again at the tall, handsome interpretive naturalist kindly and expertly giving us an engaging presentation on Yosemite transportation history. But I could not avoid hearing his voice. And if I had to give two words to describe it, I would say that from its depths and roots to its overtones, his timbre conveyed: *love* and *goodness*. As I heard his voice, I knew that he was a *good* man, and that he understood genuine, honest, real love—again, not the superficial, glamorous type of "love," but that rare vintage of love that I couldn't have recognized or heard so easily myself before taking care of Grandma and Mom. But on that note, my mind was also certain that I was not in a position to pursue a relationship at that time. My sweet mom was my greatest earthly priority, and she needed me.

Quite unaware of my internal struggle and prayers, the exceptionally attractive gentleman closed his informative history lecture. I was sad it was over, but relieved. We could leave now, and no longer would I need to be confused and resist. *Whew.* But the speaker walked a few paces over to a guitar, sat down with it, and began to strum—and sing! I didn't know what was going on, but I relaxed. To hear this man sing was not only entertaining, but comforting. Out of his mouth came, like smoky caramel, an old-timey song recalling the heyday of trains and a yearn for their return. I heard Mom's breathing slow down and deepen. Miki had fallen asleep long ago, lured by the voice of the naturalist during his presentation. Ruthie leaned back in her chair, rocked her head to the melody, and smiled. I watched as more visitors, hearing professional-quality live music, darted into the lounge from the hall and grabbed seats on the leather couches.

As soon as he was done, the enraptured audience erupted into applause and cheers. With crumpled Lincolns and Hamiltons in their hands, several listeners walked up to this newly revealed musician and expressed appreciation. I heard his modest voice give gracious thanks, and then I heard people in the audience call out "Encore!" "Sing another!"

I did a quick check of my mom. Her face was incredibly peaceful and her eyes were closed. I was going to gauge the mood of her dog, but there was not much to size up—Miki was completely asleep, half of him sprawled on my lap and the other half stretched out on Mom's lap (it seemed a little awkward, but he was apparently fine with it). Ruthie was delighted and in no rush. Having assessed my little gang and ascertained that the gentleman would be introducing another song shortly, I happily resigned myself to staying and enjoying this gift of music along with everyone else. And then, as he quietly began to pluck his guitar strings, I had an idea.

I waited, and when he had closed the second song and the audience filled the lounge with applause, I tapped Ruthie. "Can you give the speaker this tip, and ask if he can serenade my mom with 'Happy Birthday'? I can't ask him—I'm, uh—I've got Miki asleep on my and Mom's laps." I was fishing through my wallet as I said this and lamely produced the only bill I could find. Just five bucks.

"Yeah, he was really good," Ruthie agreed, going through her purse as well. She held up two dollars. "I can add this."

"His talent is worth much more than this, but it's the best we can do. I'll take care of Mom."

"I'll bring these to him," Ruthie assured me. *Whew! Now we might make tonight extra special for my Mom's birthday, AND I've managed to avoid talking to this highly attractive man.* I felt like a genius!

Mom stirred and was soon alert, so I took the opportunity to reposition a blanket over her shoulders—when I noticed something. Behind her eyeglasses, she was looking up . . . then I was suddenly aware of the sound of footsteps near us. Horrified, I slowly pivoted and raised my eyes. *Good Lord, he's walked up to us! Ruthie, what have you done! I'm gonna die!*

"I don't know 'Happy Birthday,'" he humbly apologized, guitar in one hand. "Is there some other kind of music your mom likes?"

Block out all emotion right now! Emergency mode! "Uh, do you know Josh Groban music?" I turned to smile momentarily at my mom and also to give myself a millisecond break from the intensity of directly encountering this phenomenal man. "Mom loves Josh Groban music."

NATE

"I know who he is, but I don't really know how to play his music. Is there something else she might like to hear?"

I appreciated that he was really trying to help us. "How 'bout Broadway musicals?"

"Eh," he wrinkled his nose slightly in thought. "Okay, I've got something." Pulling a chair over to us, he asked, "Have you heard of the Firefall?"

"Yeah!" I brightened. Piqued by the topic, I began to forget my nerves. "It's when that waterfall off of El Capitan reflects the winter sun and has the appearance of fire falling."

"That's right, but I meant the original Firefall."

"The original—?"

"The Firefall that you're talking about is a natural phenomenon that has only recently been a popular feature in the park. It got the name from the original Firefall, which was a manmade event based off of Glacier Point."

I felt my head tilt as my curiosity grew. "Really?"

"Yeah, so they would build a bonfire on the edge of Glacier Point. And Camp Curry—Curry Village today—is right under Glacier Point. By nine o'clock that fire would burn down to embers, and then they would push it off the edge of a cliff. From the valley, it would look like a waterfall that was made of fire. So they called it 'the Firefall.'" He smiled. I was entranced! And he continued, "As the fire fell, singers down at Camp Curry would sing this song from a musical."

"Wow. I—uh—" My eyes flitted to the people behind him, as I had become aware that there was a growing number trying to listen in. "Ah, you might want to repeat what you just said? There's people trying to hear you."

He took a quick peek over his shoulder, then stood up and addressed the little crowd, giving them a more formal version of the Firefall's backstory. I could not help but have the biggest grin on my face. This had become such a special treat for my mom, and the gentleman hadn't even sung yet. Someone asked a question. The gentleman courteously answered it, as he returned to face Mom and me and place his capo on his guitar. Someone made a comment. I responded, as our attentive speaker took the opportunity to assess the audience surrounding him and opted to scoot his chair a little closer to Mom's wheelchair.

Ruthie had my phone to take pictures, and I stroked my mom's cheek and told her, "You're getting serenaded for your birthday, Mom! He's going to sing the Firefall song for your birthday!"

I heard the strum of a guitar chord. "All set?" he asked me brightly, with a smile.

"We are!" Though feeling bashful, I couldn't help but smile back.

"All right," he said, with another strum. Then he closed his eyes and launched into a song:

> "When I'm calling you-oo-oo-oo, oo-oo-oo
> Will you answer too?-oo-oo-oo, oo-oo-oo . . ."

Gosh, this is beautiful. He's so talented.

> "That means I offer my love to you, to be your own
> If you refuse me, oh what will I do? Just wait here all alone . . ."

Wait, this is a Broadway musical song? The Firefall song? It sounds like—a love song??

> "But if you can hear my love call ringing clear
> And I hear your answering echo, so dear . . ."

Okay, this is just a performance, and he just happens to be singing a romantic country music song because it fits what we requested and he can make it sound perfect. Looking at Mom, she is so peaceful, and that's what matters. . . .

> "Then I will know our love will come true
> You'll belong to me, and I'll belong to you."

Almost at the end. Get ready to applaud and thank this fantastic, wonderful man for his great gift to my mom, and then we'll say good-bye and head our separate ways. The magic will be over, so I'd better brace myself to just move on and drown my thoughts in other things, like everything I'm responsible for.

"You'll belong to me, and I'll belong to you."[1]

The last chord was still resonating as the audience exploded into applause. I cheered! "Whoo-hoo!"

---

1. Nate's rendition is a musically significantly altered version of Friml, Harbach, and Hammerstein, "Indian Love Call." It was originally written for the musical *Rose-Marie* and was a popular hit in the 1920s.

Seemingly oblivious of the ovation surrounding him, he raised his eyebrows back at me with a smile. "Where are you guys visiting from?" The loud clapping abruptly stopped, as people silenced themselves to hear what this fine performer would do next.

Caught off guard, but wanting to honor this kind man, I answered the question. "Sacramento."

"Sacramento? Okay, nice!" he said, still smiling and nodding. Without missing a beat, he continued while taking the capo off his guitar, "So, I take it this isn't your first time to the park, then? Or is it?"

"No—I mean—growing up, Mom and Dad used to take us on family vacations here every year." I tried to stay focused on my conversation partner and not the watching crowd behind him. "It's been awhile, though, since we've—um—been to Yosemite. Came back this summer—"

"You get a little more elbow room this time of year, don't you?"

"Oh, it's amazing! It's just so different and so less crowded than in the summertime."

"Yeah, and it's kinda a shame that summertime is when everyone comes, because the scenery is probably the least dynamic that time of year." For just a second, his eyes briefly darted toward the people sitting near him, waiting for another song, yet he continued. "It's when the waterfalls are starting to dry up—um—yeah, everything's starting to dry up actually—grass, trees, and everything . . . "

Out of the corner of my vision, I saw that Mom had opened her eyes, but her able arm was active and removing her eyeglasses.

"Now, you've got fall colors."

Mom's hand rose again and removed her knit hat.

"You don't have waterfalls, but you have the fall colors, and they're beautiful depending on where you go."

"Oh my goodness, yeah."

"And then winter—you've got the snow. Spring—everything's green again. The waterfalls are booming; the dogwoods bloom in May. . . . And then, every time but Summer, just about—you have to wait 'til October's over before the crowds really go away. But, um, I'd say November through May, not counting spring break—" He finally and suddenly turned to the listeners waiting on the couch. "Is there something I can help you with?"

"We're waiting for you to sing another song," someone answered immediately and rather impatiently.

"I'm not singing anymore. I'm done for tonight," my naturalist conversationalist answered them briskly, then turned back to me. "So, November through May, not counting spring break or Christmas break, is a perfect time to be in the valley. Oh shoot—" With a slight panic on his face, he extended his guitar to me. "Here, watch this. I forgot to clock out! I'll be right back." And he ran out of the lounge.

I sat there, dumbstruck, next to my mom in her wheelchair, her dog on my lap, and this beautiful man's guitar in my hands. The remaining audience members had quickly adjourned for the night, and Ruthie had wandered over to the far side of the lounge, gazing at display cases of antique Native American basketry. I was alone for a moment with my family, feeling slightly out of place in the swanky and historied Ahwahnee Great Lounge, but not for long. He said he'd be right back, and I believed him.

A minute later, he returned. Forty-five minutes later, we were still talking but realized it was time for us all to conclude for the night. He held out his hand. "My name's Nate. What's yours?"

With a twinkle in my eye, I shook Nate's hand. "Mary."

"Good talkin' with you, Mary."

"Same."

Nate shook on a handsome black pleather and faux-fur-trimmed jacket—it was a garment that struck me as perfectly expressive of how tough, soft, and practical he was. He turned to my mom. "Happy Birthday!" he gently said to her as he bade her farewell.

Ruthie handed me my phone, and I saw that Nate had stayed an hour past his closing time. I swung my gaze up and out the ceiling-high windows of the Great Lounge. "If you run fast, you might be able to catch the last shuttle. It's dark outside—I don't think there's much moonlight."

"With these granite walls, it can take some time for the moon to show, and the cloud cover doesn't help. But—" Nate snapped a headlamp on his forehead and grinned down at me "—I'll be fine."

I laughed. "Okay then! Well, thank you again."

"You're welcome. See you again sometime."

"You, too. Good night."

"Good night."

Grabbing his guitar case and carrying a full backpack, Nate's long legs strode across the polished wooden floor, and I watched him disappear through the heavy French doors, into the night. Then I swiveled toward my mom. "Oh Mummy, let's get your glasses back on!" I said, crouching down and placing her eyeglasses lightly on her face. I reached for the knit hat in her hands. "You should be wearing your hat, too. It's time to go back to Stoneman Cottage and get some sleep!"

Two days later, we were back home in Sacramento and settled in. Miki was dozing next to my mom's feet, Ruthie was catching up with her family for a couple days, Mom was sitting propped up with a mound of pillows behind her, and I was quietly moving through her lunchtime routine.

Vitals, check. Looking great!
Pureed lunch warmed up and loaded into syringe, check.
Gloves on, check.
Position myself sitting in front of Mom, check.
A clean face towel next to tummy tube button, check.
Tummy tube opened, check.
Syringe screwed securely into place, check.
Steadily and slowly push pureed lunch through tube, che—
"I wanna go back."

It was as if the freshest wind had blown into the room, and my head bolted up. I'm pretty sure that my jaw dropped as well, but I don't remember because I was so riveted to my mom's face and the fact that she had just said a full sentence. Not only that, but her articulation was clear, even through her soft, slightly raspy voice. In addition to all this, I temporarily forgot that I was holding a syringe while I processed the fact that Mom had waited until I was sitting right there in front of her, facing her, so I wouldn't miss her words.

"You . . . wanna go back?" I repeated, to confirm that I had heard her correctly and that she meant it, though I already knew the answer. *She can only mean Yosemite, and I have a feeling she's thinking of . . . Nate.*

Mom nodded.

I tried to suppress my deep breath and gulp—I couldn't promise that we'd ever see Nate again. That was ultimately out of my hands. But I could promise one thing. "We'll go back. I promise."

15

Epilogue

Two weeks later, we did go back. And by the great grace of God, I did see Nate again. Just as he had said, November through May proved to be a perfect time to be in Yosemite valley, and not just because of the elbow room, scenery, and—as we quickly discovered—low-season pricing. And so we returned again. And again . . .

And late one night, while talking in the Ahwahnee Great Lounge after a moonlit snowshoeing hike at Badger Pass, I quietly realized that Nate was fond of me. It happened to be my birthday—though he didn't know it at the time—and it was the best birthday present I could have asked for.

On the heels of that, Mom suddenly went to ICU, and Ruthie and I scrambled to be as continuous a presence for my mom as the staff would allow. I did not know if I would ever see Nate again. However, barring an extended snowstorm (which was a very real possibility), Nate determined to drive hours through winter mountain conditions to spend the day with Mom and me at a very urban hospital. He brought his guitar to play and sing for Mom; he hand-delivered salted caramel cookies he had baked for me and Ruthie; and shortly before he tackled the unlit, snow-covered forest roads back to Yosemite in his hardy pickup truck, he broke out his little red Orthodox prayer book and interceded for Mom's healing. A couple weekends later, Nate returned, and he came back the weekend after that, and the weekend after that. The days were hard, but the load was lighter with the support of this gentle, compassionate, and strong man who had come alongside us.

EPILOGUE

After several weeks, Mom had improved sufficiently enough that the hospital made plans for her to return home. But unexpectedly, two days before she was going to be discharged, her health made a sudden turn for the worse and she was forced to return to ICU instead of home. Very sadly, things went downhill quickly from there. Ben managed to travel back home in time to say goodbye to Mom at her bedside. Miki was given special permission to be carried into Mom's hospital room and placed on her bed, her hand feeling his soft coat one more time. And too soon, one cold March morning in ICU, after Ruthie, Auntie Bev, and I clutched each other, sobbing, Nate rushed in from Yosemite with his guitar, hoping to bring some sort of solace or comfort if he could. Instead, he found himself in tears at my mother's bedside as he struggled momentarily to find the words to pray.

For Miki, the loss of his affectionate and ever-present alpha—my mom—was a grief that drove him to somewhere between depression and paranoia that he would lose me as well. However, God knows (and, I'm quite certain, Mom did as well) that both Miki's and my hearts received the balm of Nate's sensitive and caring presence in our lives. And when Nate and I married, the move to the sylvan mountains near Yosemite proved to be healing for Mom's young-at-heart dog. Her little white dream dog became our fur baby, and he has spent many hours sleeping near my desk as I've prayed and written my way through this memoir. Even now, as I'm writing these words, Miki is just a few feet away, snuggled up on his makeshift dog bed of a pillow and throw that Mom and he often shared together.

Meanwhile, Nate continues to educate visitors about the rich natural and cultural history of Yosemite National Park, now through a sustainable, local co-operative. In addition to introducing people to the iconic valley that he treasures, he is in the midst of training to guide fishing excursions throughout the region in gorgeous wilderness places that, without fail, have always sent my man home to me in a renewed and refreshed state of mind and heart. Though Nate's fly-fishing acumen is not in the simple, dilettante realm of my beloved grandmother's kind of fishing, I have no doubt that Grandma would have delighted in Nate's fishing skills if she were still walking among us. Certainly, both Grandma and Mom would have rejoiced in every fish Nate brings home and would have been proud to clean, cook, and, of course, eat their favorite meat. I am also confident that Mom would have been touched and impressed with the gardening and landscaping skills that Nate developed in order to restore and grow her garden after she passed away. Joyfully predictably, my husband took these abilities to our own home and applied them to his signature areas of interest, growing native plants and building his own deer-proof crop cages for vegetables.

Near where we pray together daily, opening and closing the day, is a newspaper clipping matted and framed by my husband. It's an account of my grandparents' love story and journey to America. And many nights after we pray, when Mom's favored sun has gone down to rest and Grandma's captivating moon is hiding its face, I scoop up the little dog at my feet and Nate takes us outside to look at the stars. I look for the Milky Way; he looks for the four handfuls of stars that he knows by name. He points out to me the seasonal planets and steers me toward galaxies—fascinating smudges of light in the night sky. And sometimes I find it interesting that Grandma liked the moon; Mom, the sun; and Nate, he gazes at the stars. But to be fair, Nate attends to much more than the starry sky. He'll take it all—sun, moon, stars, galaxies, trees, mountains, low-lying stream, high country lake, rainbow trout, brown trout, brook trout, tiny tadpoles at our feet after we paddle our kayak to shore, frost, cracking thunder, blizzard, graupel, giant sequoia, Lilliputian-sized sequoia seed shaken from a smooth-scaled cone, silver bush lupine, acorn woodpecker, Steller's jays that mimic red-shouldered hawks, checkerspot butterfly, glacial cirque, raven nest, the clicks and chirps of bats (which are quite fond of the towering non-native redwood trees in our backyard) . . . You name it in these forested mountains that God has so graced, my husband will take nearly all of it in just about every season but the scorching wildfire-prone one that summer has become. Even without the sun or the moon, we can handle it.

"Babe, do you have to cover the plants now? It's pretty dark outside, and there's three mountain lions in our neighborhood."
"I'll be fine—I know what to do. You should, too! And I've got my headlamp."

"Ahh! Nate! Power's out!"
"I can see that. Let's light the candles and oil lamps."
"Okay. I'll grab some snacks and a blanket. Let's go outside!"

But just last week . . .

"Mary! Mary!"
"Babe, I'm here! What's going on? Why aren't you at work?"

EPILOGUE

"I was, but a wildfire just broke out on the edge of town, and I knew that you're keeping your phone off while you're finishing your book. I did try to call you, but it wouldn't go through, of course. You remember our evacuation plan? . . . "

Obviously, no one is thrilled to be living ten minutes away from a wildfire, but I am thankful for my vigilant husband, who knows me so well and cares about me so much that he would drop his work preparations to assure that his wife is alert and ready to evacuate regardless of whether or not she was foolish enough to have her phone off during wildfire season (it's on now, but in silent mode).

In the ebb and flow of our many close interactions with the created order, as if to remind me metaphorically of the significance of those who have loved us and gone before us, I happened to notice just last night the unusual brightness of the moon when I took Miki outside before bedtime. I was so struck by its appearance that I called out to Nate through the window to come see it.

"It's a super moon," Nate informed me.

Not only that, it was a rare super blue moon, viewed on the second night of its three-day tenure. We also saw it the first night while truck camping in the eastern Sierra. As it rose, Nate remarked on how beautiful it was (and I covered my sleepy eyes with a shirt sleeve because the moonlight streaming into the truck was so bright). But we did not know then that it was also an unusual phenomenon. Completing the final manuscript for this book in the midst of a three-day, rare, exceptionally luminous-and-large moon episode . . . A blessed coincidence?

As Grandma would say, God knows. Yes indeed, Grandma—God knows. And I'm so grateful He does.

A gift by Nate's godson, Atlas, at ten years of age

Postscript

Two days after finishing my manuscript, I was informed that my paternal uncle was in hospice. As if a wildfire was approaching, I went on go-bag mode, grabbed Miki, and drove nearly non-stop for eight hours to Escondido to see my uncle and help my cousins navigate the challenges and opportunities of giving care to a loved one at home in hospice (it turned out that they were doing such a great job that the privilege was simply mine to be there). Meanwhile, Nate, stuck at home with Covid, arranged accommodations for me and Miki and kept me company on the drive via our cell phones.

The next morning, I was greeted on my uncle's doorstep by my cousin Luis. In between catching some special moments with Uncle Albert throughout the day, my cousins and I would rest and refresh in the kitchen—that age-old domestic locale of family nurture and interaction. Many precious and irreplaceable memories and ruminations were passed across the mosaic café table while Uncle slept peacefully under our vigils. And one in particular from Cousin Luis resonated in a lovely way with a theme of this memoir. Now in his years of wisdom, Luis has maintained long and affectionate relationships with his children, similar to that of Grandma and me. With tears in his eyes and a voice that nearly cracked, Luis looked up at me and remarked that he loves the moon—he loves the beauty of the moon, and he loved to share such admiration of it with his daughter Alexis. Sometimes, when he was elsewhere from his daughter and saw a remarkable moon, he would think, *Wow, that is so beautiful!* and would send a message to her phone: "Have you seen the moon tonight?"

This was such a cherished interaction between father and daughter that Alexis honored it by giving it flesh and bone. She gave her first child—Luis' first grandchild—the name Luna.

Acknowledgments

MANY THANKS ARE DUE to several special people for the completion of this book:

Patsy Theodora and Jonathan Porphyrios, who both asked just the right questions at just the right time during the writing of this memoir (and stuck around to hear the whole story!). Sh. Yolanda, whose prayers, friendship, and gentle wisdom made a difference. Myriah Mary, Atlas George, and Penny Anysia, for your enthusiasm and artistic talent.

Lyn, Megan, Onesimus, Jennifer, Vanessa, and my husband Nate, for your encouragement and helpful comments on earlier versions of my manuscript. It's been quite a journey in both life and writing, and I am especially appreciative to Vanessa for her thoughtful presence and coaching through a significant part of it.

Matt, George, Ian, Karlie, Savanah, and the Wipf and Stock gang, for being a blessed joy to work with again. Thank you for welcoming this project and wasting no time in giving it wings. I remain deeply grateful for both the expertise and humanity with which you guide your authors, and I am proud to be counted among them.

Fr. Ian, for encouraging me to finish this book. The Cooling family, for the same as well as their long and valued friendship. Emeka and Amarachi, for your prayers, friendship, and inspiring examples of faith, courage, wisdom, and love over the long haul (also, on a less profound but memorable note, for introducing me to my first legit mosquito nets).

Aunt Lois, Uncle Tim, and Grandma Mary Strauss, for so generously opening your home to us (Miki included) while I attended to my uncle in hospice and worked on the final stages of my manuscript.

My very sweet and faith-full mom, who supported and took seriously my love of writing at a young age. Her sacrificial love and care for her family, friends, and community were beyond the pages of this book, and I have

Acknowledgments

no doubt that she prayed innumerable prayers that God used to shape me, my life, and my work.

Auntie Clarinda, Uncle Arnold, Auntie Bev, and Uncle Alan, for caring for us like surrogate family in our Lord. We needed you all, and you were there. Thank you for your incredible love and support through every season.

Dad Tom and Mom Beryl, for welcoming me and Miki into the Smith family so joyfully and warmly. Thank you for your prayers and care for all of us, regardless of the geographical distance.

And most of all, my husband, Nate, without whom this book might not have gotten finished and surely without whom the tone of my writing and the very chapters of my life lately would lack several degrees of *shalom*. Thank you, babe, for proving again and again—though there has never been any need to prove anything; this is simply how thoroughly and deeply you are this way—that you are God's greatest gift to me.

Bibliography

Basil of Caesarea. "The Creation of Luminous Bodies." In *Hexæmeron*. Translated by Blomfield Jackson. In *Basil: Letters and Select Works*. Vol. 8 of *A Select Library of the Nicene and Post-Nicene Fathers of The Christian Church*, 2nd ser., edited by Philip Schaff and Henry Wace. New York: Christian Literature Co., 1890–1900. Reprint, Edinburgh: T & T Clark; Grand Rapids: Eerdmans, 1988–1991.

Friml, Rudolf, Otto Harbach, and Oscar Hammerstein II. "Indian Love Call," *Rose-Marie*. New York: Harms, 1924.

MARY KATHERINE Y. H. HOM-SMITH (PhD, University of Cambridge) is a freelance academic and author. A former assistant professor of biblical studies, she has published in various scholarly journals (including *Vetus Testamentum, Novum Testamentum, Journal of Biblical Literature, Biblische Notizen,* and *Journal of the Adventist Theological Society*), lectured and taught in numerous countries on five continents, and been featured in several biblical studies podcast interviews. She is also the author of *The Characterization of an Empire* (Wipf & Stock) and *The Characterization of the Assyrians in Isaiah* (LHBOTS, T&T Clark). She and her husband, Nate, reside in the mountains of California with their little dog, Miki, and have been active participants in their parish's Orthodox church.

www.ingramcontent.com/pod-product-compliance
Lightning Source LLC
Chambersburg PA
CBHW062220080426
42734CB00010B/1966